Hiking Trails in Valles Caldera
National Preserve

Hiking Trails

IN Valles Caldera

National Preserve

REVISED EDITION

COCO RAE

FOREWORD BY TOM RIBE

University of New Mexico Press | Albuquerque

ISBN 978-0-8263-6360-2 (paper)
ISBN 978-0-8263-6361-9 (e-book)

Library of Congress Control Number: 2021952524

Founded in 1889, the University of New Mexico sits on the traditional homelands of the Pueblo of Sandia. The original peoples of New Mexico—Pueblo, Navajo, and Apache—since time immemorial have deep connections to the land and have made significant contributions to the broader community statewide. We honor the land itself and those who remain stewards of this land throughout the generations and also acknowledge our committed relationship to Indigenous peoples. We gratefully recognize our history.

Cover photograph by Coco Rae
Title page photograph courtesy of Peter Dickson
Designed by Felicia Cedillos
Composed in Charter 9.5/14.25

The Leave No Trace Seven Principles by the Leave No Trace Center for Outdoor
    Ethics, www.LNT.org, © 1999. Used with permission.
GPS tracks and GPX data generated using Gaia GPS for iOS. Used with
    permission.
Maps generated using CalTopo. Used with permission.
USFS 2013 map layer generated using United States Forest Service open-source
    data.
Photographs by Peter Dickson appear with his permission. Photograph by NASA
    Earth Observatory (page 7) is an open-source satellite image of Valles Caldera
    created by Jesse Allen and Robert Simmon using Landsat data provided by
    the United States Geological Survey, 2002. All other photographs are by the
    author.

To Brittney and Dave,
who got me started

CONTENTS

Looking west across Valle Grande from Cañada Bonita Trail, Pajarito Mountain Ski Area, Los Alamos. Photo by Peter Dickson.

FOREWORD

It is difficult to overstate the beauty and the centrality of the Valles
Caldera to this place we call New Mexico. Seen from space, this now
quiet volcano looks like the footprint of a great bear, who stepped
here and nowhere else on some unseen journey. In a region filled
with mountains, this place leaves those who see it for the first time
stunned by its grandeur and its vast sense of time. We are but the
latest people who have passed here over thousands of years, trailing
among the great meadows, forests, and streams that reach away
across this most sacrosanct of regions.

Valles Caldera National Preserve (VCNP) is the center of the
Jemez Mountains, a volcanic range whose great violent expression
of stone and ash more than a million years ago transformed the area
and ultimately created a gentle range of mountains and mesas, hos-
pitable to the people who built their villages and traditions around
the base of the volcano's remains. These mountains teem with animals and the ghosts of more stories than we can ever know from a
variety of peoples who have come here to be changed by this place.
From archaic times when people gathered the obsidian scattered
like fragments of night across the land, to today's scientists who
seek understanding, to the elk who look across fields of flowers in
summer rain, to friends on an afternoon walk of discovery, to Pueblo
peoples in ceremony, this place opens itself to us, a great cathedral of
mystery.

I've known this place my whole life, from childhood trips on the
highway through the gaping Valle Grande, to secret night trespasses
in adolescence where we gazed into a universe of stars through giant
Douglas firs and wondered at the opening universe within ourselves.

We found the calypso orchid at the bases of blue spruce and heard the coyotes call from the deeper wilds. And I've watched the toll years take on a place as the wet, beautiful forests of my childhood have been ravaged by high-severity fire, and places once cool and shaded are opened to slow recovery that will take generations and will reach an uncertain ecological end point.

I recall my first legal trip in 1991 into the private Baca Ranch with commissioners from the New Mexico Public Regulatory Commission, who wanted to see for themselves what the large, contemplated Ojo Line Extension power line would destroy were it built across this landscape. It never was, and that fact allowed greater futures to be considered once the property was purchased by the American people in 2000. More recently, I recall a trip through the preserve in 2014 with Senator Martin Heinrich and the current superintendent of the preserve, as the senator wrangled legislation to move the Valles Caldera under the National Park Service (NPS), which now manages this land on behalf of the American people.

Valles Caldera National Preserve is a rare site in the Southwest national park system, as it is dedicated primarily to protection of the natural world, rather than grand cultural resources. There are cultural sites here such as obsidian, active Pueblo shrines, and historic cabins. Yet the preserve offers an opportunity to manage this landscape for recreation, restoration, and research, according to the mission of the National Park Service.

Already the preserve's partner groups have restored wetlands, planted willows, removed old fencing, and stopped erosion that began when domestic sheep grazed the area to dust in the 1930s. And NPS has undertaken a multiyear forest restoration project meant to reverse damage caused by logging and fire suppression, which left the land vulnerable to high-severity fire. They have reintroduced moderate-severity fire to the grasslands and forests, boosting the diversity of species and inoculating the land against future wildfire. The preserve is largely closed to livestock grazing so the grasslands and streams can at last recover from a century of overgrazing.

Even so, scars of recent high-severity fires are all too apparent in the preserve. The 156,000-acre Las Conchas Fire started when a tree hit an electrical line on June 26, 2011, and burned 44,000 acres on its first day. It burned along the southern and eastern rims of Valle Grande and into upper Bandelier National Monument and Cochiti Canyon, where it burned at great intensity. The 2013 Thompson Ridge Fire burned 15,000 acres on Redondo and South Mountains, as a mixed-severity fire. Today you can see the recovering scars of both these fires, and scientists at the preserve are measuring the link between such fires and climate change.

Today the Jemez Mountains and the Valles Caldera in particular are the most scientifically studied landscape in the Southwest, and this research guides management decisions while providing insight into the workings of this mysterious landscape. In a sense, this is a great laboratory of climate, wildlife, geology, paleoecology, and fire ecology, aptly just over the ridge from Los Alamos National Laboratory.

Yet through all the science and management, Valles Caldera National Preserve ultimately yields a wonderful mix of experiences in this young volcanic landscape to its owners, the American people. It's possible to drive, hike, bicycle, ski, snowshoe, horseback ride, fish, and hunt. You can look for birds, flowers, bears, rocks, and insights. Exert yourself in great beauty or relax in the tall grass and while away your afternoon. Coco's guidebook provides previously unavailable guidance to the trailheads and trails that deepen our experience of a place, drawing us into this unique world that will nurture our spirits.

Here we have a healing landscape, inviting us to walk its trails or stride across its great meadows. Coco's guidebook opens a world of opportunity, a lifetime of day hikes to be done again and again in the high New Mexico air.

Tom Ribe, author of *Inferno by Committee: A History of the Cerro Grande (Los Alamos) Fire, America's Worst Prescribed Fire Disaster*

PREFACE

This guidebook developed out of a project I undertook as part of my volunteer work at Valles Caldera National Preserve (VCNP). Since coming under the management of the National Park Service in 2014, the staff of the preserve have undertaken the Sisyphean task of restoring and protecting a landscape that has suffered from fire, drought, overgrazing, and destructive logging. Additionally, they have been working to improve the public's access to all that makes this land so special. While the preserve has over 1,000 miles of timber roads, the majority are being allowed to return to nature as part of the restoration process. Those that remain, designated as official trails, lacked documentation of conditions, signage, and in some cases even accurate mileage measurements. At the same time, there was no comprehensive guide to the official trails of the preserve, much to the dismay of hikers and bikers who want to explore the backcountry. Over the course of about eighteen months, I set out to hike each of the official trails, mapping them using Gaia GPS, documenting trail conditions, and producing reports on each that could be used by the preserve staff in their ongoing infrastructure work. About halfway through the project, I realized I had enough information to write the guidebook that I and all my fellow hikers and bikers have been wishing for. The result is the book you have in your hands. I hope it will help you to explore and enjoy the preserve for many years to come.

If you want to contribute to ongoing improvements at the preserve, there are many ways to get involved:

Volunteers-in-Parks (VIPs). This is one of the best ways to contribute to the preserve, and there are opportunities for every interest. Visit www.nps.gov/getinvolved/volunteer.htm for more information. Sign up for VCNP volunteer opportunities at www.volunteer.gov.

Los Amigos de Valles Caldera. The preserve's official Friends group. In addition to managing the preserve's bookstore, they organize a variety of tours, sponsor special events, and support projects such as wetland restoration. To learn more, visit www.losamigosdevallescaldera.org.

Caldera Action. A citizens' group focused on the protection and preservation of VCNP. They were instrumental in gaining support for the National Park Service's management plan, and they continue to work with community members, New Mexico's congressional delegation, and VCNP leadership. To get involved, visit www.caldera-action.org.

Trail updates. If you hike or bike one of these trails and discover conditions have changed, please email me at vcnp.trails@gmail.com. Include specifics of the change (new signage, washout, etc.), trail name and location (coordinates if possible), photograph(s), and date. Useful contributions will be acknowledged in the next edition of this guide.

Note: This guidebook is not affiliated in any way with the National Park Service, the Sierra Club, or Leave No Trace and the Center for Outdoor Ethics. Any opinions expressed herein are solely those of the author.

ACKNOWLEDGMENTS

This trail guide would have remained little more than scribbled notes in my backpack without the knowledge, advice, and assistance of many people. First and foremost, thanks go to the amazing staff and volunteers at Valles Caldera National Preserve, especially Kimberly DeVall, for all of the backcountry permissions and trails access; Dave Jones, for putting up with me during our shared shifts and offering his wisdom with a twinkle in his eye; Seth Gayner and Nate Plants, for advice and reports on trail conditions as well as tales of hikes gone wrong; Sue Anderson, for always being good for a laugh; Dan Kish and Emily Guss, for supporting this project wholeheartedly; and the many wonderful fellow volunteers with whom I have worked and who reviewed my trail reports. Enormous thanks also go to Brittney Van Der Werff, formerly of VCNP, for taking me on as a volunteer and for her friendship.

I am indebted to the Northern New Mexico Group of the Sierra Club, whose classic guidebook *Day Hikes in the Santa Fe Area* has taken me all over New Mexico's backcountry and has inspired me to write this guide. Special thanks go to Aku Oppenheimer, who graciously reviewed a draft of this guidebook.

Much gratitude also goes to the many friends and family members who contributed to the production of this guide. First, my deepest appreciation goes to my dearest hiking buddies Rob Weiner and James Taylor, who reviewed the trail descriptions and offered countless helpful suggestions. Next, thanks go to Peter Dickson, who shared his photos and advice regarding mountain bike routes; to Leanna Kiksuyapi Dawn McClure, who reviewed the details of local Native American history; to my brother Ním Wunnan, who made the cover and photos presentable for the first edition; and to my parents, who edited and proofed far too many drafts. I am also extremely grateful to the folks at University of New Mexico Press, who saw the value of this work and wanted to bring it to a wider audience, and who put together this beautiful new revised edition. Any errors or omissions are solely my own.

Lastly, heartfelt thanks go to my husband Philip, who (mostly) willingly hiked nearly all of the trails with me, and without whom none of this would have been possible.

Coco Rae
Los Alamos, 2022
Revised Edition

Accessing Valles Caldera National Preserve

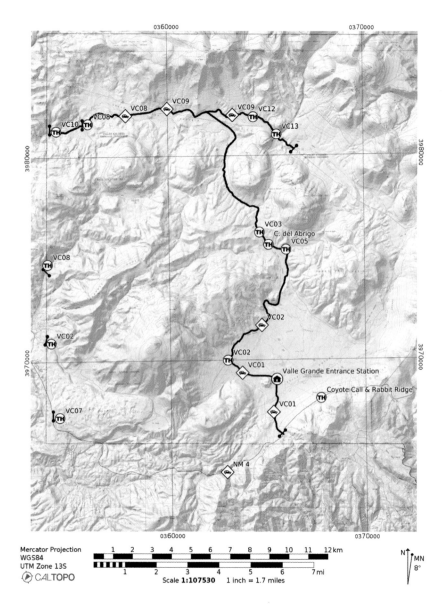

Mercator Projection
WGS84
UTM Zone 13S

CALTOPO

Scale **1:107530**   1 inch = 1.7 miles

N ↑ MN 8°

Accessing Valles Caldera National Preserve

Valles Caldera National Preserve is located near mile marker 39 on the north side of NM 4 in Sandoval County, about 30 minutes west of Los Alamos. The map on page 2 illustrates the backcountry access roads, along which most trailheads are located. The trailheads for Coyote Call & Rabbit Ridge Trails, Banco Bonito Loop (VC07), and Redondo Creek–Mirror Pond Trail (VC02) are accessed directly from NM 4. The trailhead for Sulfur & Alamo Canyons Loop and Redondo Border Trail (VC08) is accessed from Forest Road 105, which is near mile marker 27 on NM 4. It takes about 90 minutes to reach VCNP from either Santa Fe or Albuquerque, depending on traffic and weather conditions.

Driving directions from Santa Fe: Take US 84/285 north to Pojoaque and turn left (west) onto NM 502. Take NM 502 to the exit for NM 4 and follow the signs for Bandelier National Monument and White Rock. At the stoplight at the T-junction, turn right (west) to take NM 501/East Jemez Road (the Los Alamos truck route) up the hill. At the stoplight at the top of the hill, turn left (south) to pass through the security checkpoint at Los Alamos National Laboratory (LANL). This generally only requires you to show your driver's license, and is necessary because the road passes through LANL property. Follow the signs along NM 501 as it passes through the laboratory and turns south, reaching a T-junction with NM 4. Turn right (west) onto NM 4 and head up the mountain, reaching the entrance gate for VCNP after about 10 miles.

If you do not wish to pass through the LANL security checkpoint, instead of taking NM 501/East Jemez Road up the hill, continue on

NM 4 through White Rock, following the signs for Bandelier National Monument. Continue past the entrance to Bandelier, taking NM 4 all the way to VCNP. This route is slightly longer but avoids the checkpoint.

Driving directions from Albuquerque: Take I-25 north to Bernalillo to the exit for US 550. Turn left (west) onto US 550 and take it north to San Ysidro. At San Ysidro, turn right (northeast) onto NM 4. Follow NM 4 as it heads up the mountain, reaching the entrance gate for VCNP after about 39 miles.

A Brief History of Valles Caldera National Preserve

Valles Caldera National Preserve is one of the newest of the protected lands within the National Park System, yet its landscape reflects a political history of centuries, a cultural history of thousands of years, and a geological history of millions of years. In its past we may see traces of Spain's New World empire, Mexico's fight for independence, America's westward expansion, and New Mexico's integration into the United States. One may also see the long and rich history of Native American life and culture in the Southwest and its extensive ties to far-flung Indigenous communities across North America. And of course, the geological forces that shaped the landscape as we know it today may be read in the hills and valleys that make up this unique and special place.

The geological history of VCNP has been a source of fascination for thousands of visitors, and it has established the caldera as a must-see destination for professional and amateur geologists from all over the world. Indeed, Fraser Goff (2009), one of the leading experts on the caldera's geology, has noted that it is "the world's best example of a resurgent caldera," having been identified as a caldera in the 1920s by C. S. Ross of the United States Geological Survey. The caldera is so well defined that in the 1960s, geologists R. L. Smith and R. A. Bailey decided to use its characteristics to define all calderas worldwide (Goff 2009). The preserve sits atop the junction of two major geological features of the Southwest: the Jemez Lineament, which runs southwest to northeast across New Mexico, and the Rio Grande Rift, which runs north to south down the middle of the state. The Jemez Lineament is easy to see on a map of the Southwest. Its presence may be traced from Arizona's White Mountains in the southwest, across the caldera, and up to Capulin Volcano in the Raton–Clayton volcanic field in the northeast corner of New Mexico. Similarly, the Rio Grande Rift is marked by the famous river that flows down it. For millions of years, these tectonic features have produced a wide variety of volcanic activity, perhaps the most spectacular being the two major eruptions that created the caldera.

When viewed from above, the caldera is slightly oval in appearance, rather than more perfectly round; this is because the first major eruption, which created the Toledo Caldera around 1.6 million years ago, was nearly obliterated by the second eruption, which created the current caldera rim around 1.25 million years ago (Goff 2009). Caldera formation may be understood as something like a magma-filled soufflé: As rifts pull apart and temperatures and pressures rise, the land is forced upward by the rising magma, until the pressure becomes so great that an eruption occurs, scattering volcanic material everywhere. When the pressure is released and the magma is spent, what material remains collapses and the center drops lower than its original surface, filling the void left behind by the erupting lava. The Toledo Caldera was approximately 9 miles in diameter. It developed after producing an eruption column nearly 20 miles high, pyroclastic flows of 50–200 miles per hour and at least 950° F, and 85 cubic miles of volcanic material that reached as far as what is now Kansas (Goff 2009). Within about 400,000 years of the Toledo Caldera eruption, the first lava dome, Rabbit Mountain, formed along the southern rim. A lava dome is formed by a secondary, lesser eruption, whereby magma rises to the surface and erupts as lava, which subsequently hardens to form a volcanic dome.

The second major eruption, which created the rim of the caldera as we know it today, produced slightly less volcanic material, yielding about 75 cubic miles of ash flow and scattering it nearly as far as the Toledo eruption (Goff 2009). For comparison, the famous 1980 eruption of Mount St. Helens only yielded 0.7 cubic miles of debris. However, although both eruptions were impressive, despite popular belief

Satellite image of Valles Caldera. Photo by NASA Earth Observatory.

the caldera is not a supervolcano, the definition of which requires over 240 cubic miles of debris. The resultant oval ring produced by the second eruption is about 12–15 miles in diameter, depending on where it is measured. Of the three large Quaternary period calderas (2.58 million years ago to today) in the United States—Yellowstone in Wyoming, Long Valley in California, and Valles Caldera—Valles Caldera is the oldest and the smallest (Goff 2009). The ash deposits of the first eruption are known as Lower Bandelier Tuff, and the ash deposits of the second eruption are known as Upper Bandelier Tuff. Both of these layers may be seen in the mesas of the nearby Pajarito and Jemez Plateaus, and it is out of Upper Bandelier Tuff that the ancient Pueblo peoples enlarged air pockets into cave dwellings and ultimately expanded into the built structures that may be seen at nearby Bandelier National Monument.

Soon after the second eruption the valley floor began to rise again, and in the incredibly brief period of about 30,000 years, Redondo Mountain was formed at a rate of about 1 inch per year. Goff (2009) notes that, had people been living in the area at the time, this rate was fast enough to have been noticeable. This is the highest of the mountains within the caldera, reaching 11,254 feet, which is roughly the height of the highest point before the original eruption. Redondo Mountain is the only resurgent dome in the preserve, which means the magma forced the surface upward but did not actually erupt. After Redondo Mountain formed, a series of further eruptions occurred over about 750,000 years, forming lava domes starting with Cerro del Medio around 1.23 million years ago, and erupting roughly counterclockwise one by one until San Antonio Mountain was formed around 560,000 years ago. Cerro La Jara, the tiny dome adjacent to the VCNP Entrance Station, and South Mountain, just to the north of it, were both formed around 520,000 years ago. The El Cajete formation occurred around 55,000 years ago, and the Banco Bonito formation is the youngest in the preserve, having developed around 40,000 years ago (Goff 2009). As these lava domes formed, they filled in the floor of the caldera, delimiting the many valleys within it that may be explored today. While volcanic activity has been minimal since the Banco Bonito eruption, the caldera is not considered to be extinct. It is known that a magma chamber exists about 4.5 miles below the surface (Goff 2009), hot springs and fumaroles may be seen on the western side of the preserve and down to the community of Jemez Springs, and tiny earthquakes are measured on a regular basis.

After the second eruption the caldera lacked any outflow, resulting in a lake that quickly formed due to rainfall and underground springs. Over thousands of years and many subsequent eruptions there were at least four periods of time when the caldera floor was

Looking east across Valle Grande.

filled with water (Goff 2009). Erosion and eruptions eventually shifted the landscape such that today, the caldera's creeks, springs, and the East Fork of the Jemez River drain the caldera, ultimately emptying into the Rio Grande. The prehistoric lakes are partly the reason why there are no trees on the valley floors today: the lake sediment stretches nearly 300 feet below the surface (Goff 2009), and its density and mineral content are not conducive to the growth of the Douglas fir, aspen, and ponderosa typical of the region. Additionally, the valleys' lower elevations act as a cold sink, with the result that there are too many days below freezing over the course of a year to allow seedlings to take hold. The inverse tree line of the caldera is one of the preserve's many unique features, and the meadows of its valleys are what have made the area so attractive to the peoples who have lived in the region.

Archaeological data suggest that the first human presence in the caldera dates to approximately 12,000 years ago (Anschuetz and Merlan 2007). The first peoples of the region appear to have spent time in the caldera in seasonal camps, attracted by the superb quality of the obsidian as well as the extensive variety of plants and animals. Production sites of obsidian arrowheads, spearheads, and other tools, as well as major quarries, have been documented around the preserve, and obsidian from here has been found as far away as North Dakota and Mississippi (NPS 2018), indicating extensive trade connections with other Native American communities of the Americas. More than 350 species of plants have been identified that were (and are) used for both medicinal and spiritual purposes (Anschuetz and Merlan 2007). By about 600 AD, permanent settlements bearing distinctly Pueblo characteristics, including pottery and arrowheads, had begun to develop in the region. After about 1350 AD, when the settlement of Chaco Canyon, the cultural and political heart of the Southwest, had been abandoned, the population in the Jemez Mountains began to increase and the distinctive, multi-room Pueblo villages began to develop (Anschuetz and Merlan 2007). It was also around this time that the Banco Bonito field houses were built. These are small rectangular structures, usually with one room, that were used during the growing season for shelter. Their presence is testimony to the ingenuity of the agricultural practices of the Native American peoples in the region, as these fields for corn and squash are the highest elevation example of farming currently known (Martin 2003).

Many modern Native American communities in the region have ancestral ties to the caldera, particularly Jemez Pueblo and Zia Pueblo, but also including nearly all the Pueblos of New Mexico, as well as the Jicarilla Apache, Ute, and Diné (Navajo). Still other Native American communities throughout the Southwest also trace their history to the area (NPS 2018). Archaeologists and anthropologists connect some of these modern communities to the peoples who arrived after 1350, but it is important to recognize that Native American communities have their own histories of themselves and their own understanding of their ties to the caldera, both of which are equally valid and form a

A fine example of an obsidian scraper tool. Leave artifacts where you find them.

complementary narrative to the history of the region. In their land-use history of VCNP, archaeologist and anthropologist Kurt Anschuetz and historian Thomas Merlan note that

> [these] communities understand themselves to be integral parts of a living historical-ecological process in which the people are as much of a part of the land as the land is part of the people over time. Communities project their sense of soul onto the Valles Caldera landscape. The Valles Caldera, therefore, is more than a geographic place that communities visited to obtain various material resources. It is an essential part of peoples' histories and cultural identities. . . . Communities associate the mountains, springs, caves, shrines, streams, and the hollow of the Valle Grande with a borderland where the sky, the earth, and underworld intersect. The Valles Caldera is a place of power because it is a location where the objective world (i.e., the earth) meets the subjective realms of the cosmos (i.e., the heavens and the underworld). . . . The Valles Caldera is a symbol of a community's cultural traditions and history that informs the people of "how they became who they are." (Anschuetz and Merlan 2007)

It is for these and other, unspoken reasons that the caldera remains so sacred. Indeed, when one sees the outline of the Jemez Mountains rising above the surrounding plains, it takes little imagination to understand why the caldera figures so large in the traditions of so many of the surrounding Native American communities. In particular, the centrality of Redondo Mountain to local Native American history is deeply connected to its sacredness; visitors are asked to respect this and not attempt to summit its peak.

With the sixteenth century came the Spanish, and it is thought that a party tied to Don Juan de Oñate, to this day a profoundly divisive figure in the region, may have been the first Europeans to cross the caldera in the early seventeenth century on their way to explore the regions west of their settlement near what is now Española (Martin 2003). While the valleys with their rich grasses were certainly

12

View of Redondo Mountain from NM 4.

appealing to the Spanish for the sheep, cattle, and horses they had introduced to the region, the remoteness of the caldera from Spanish settlements, the sheer difficulty of accessing it, and the incredibly short growing season, as well as what is often euphemistically termed "unsettled relations" with Indigenous tribes, meant very little Spanish presence until the early nineteenth century. It is marked as "Valle de los Bacas" (Valley of the Cows) on a 1779 map and eventually came to be called, simply, "Los Valles" (the Valleys) (Martin 2003).

In 1821, the Cabeza de Baca family was granted half a million acres near what is now Las Vegas, New Mexico, by the Spanish government. A number of issues made it difficult for them to occupy the land, including trespassing shepherds, illicit fur trappers from Canadian and American territories, Pawnee raids, and increasingly large squatter settlements. By 1835 the now Mexican provincial government in Santa Fe had granted the land to thirty settlers, in the belief that the Baca family had abandoned it (Martin 2003). Before the

Baca family could resolve their claim, however, international events intervened, with the American invasion and occupation of New Mexico in 1846 during the Mexican–American War. The 1848 Treaty of Guadalupe Hidalgo, which ended the war, included a provision that required all land grants issued by either the Spanish or Mexican governments to be reviewed and validated or repudiated by the American government. Part of the reason for this provision was that, under both Spanish and Mexican law, land could be held in common by whole families and their descendants or by a community comprised of multiple families; on the other hand, Anglo-American law stated that land and property were held individually. This fundamental difference in the legal definition of ownership would have profound and often devastating implications for Hispanic families and communities in New Mexico as land-hungry Americans from back east moved into their newly acquired territory.

After the war ended, the Baca family sought to press their claim against the growing community of Las Vegas. In 1860 the US Surveyor General found both claims to be valid, but as the town of Las Vegas could not be removed from its location, the Bacas were offered their pick of five 100,000-acre parcels in the Southwest. Their first choice, Baca Location No. 1, encompassed the caldera, and indeed the name still appears on modern maps. Location No. 2 was near what is now Tucumcari, New Mexico; Locations No. 3 and No. 5 were near Nogales and Prescott, Arizona, respectively; and Location No. 4 was in the San Luis Valley in southern Colorado. However, John Watts, the lawyer hired by the Bacas to argue their case, received Location Nos. 2, 3, and 4 in payment, and by 1871 he had purchased Location No. 5 (Martin 2003). Finally, in 1876, title to Location No. 1 was legally recorded after a survey completed in the astounding time of four days confirmed the boundary lines (it would later be shown that the 1876 survey lines were short by 10,000 acres) (Martin 2003).

Like most New Mexicans at the time, the Baca family ran sheep on their land, sharing the resources of the grazing lands among the many grantees' families and their neighbors. This was a tradition that had developed out of the community land-grant system and which

View of Obsidian Valley from Cerros del Abrigo Loop (77).

enabled shareholders to support their families in the unforgiving
environment of northern New Mexico. Summer sheep camps were
established in Valle San Antonio, Valle Toledo, and Valle de los Posos
(Martin 2003). However, the last quarter of the nineteenth century
in New Mexico saw rampant land speculation as unscrupulous lawyers (mostly Anglo, but sometimes in partnership with influential
Hispanic families) exploited to their advantage the peculiarities of
land-grant inheritances and the American legal definition of ownership, as well as the inability of most landowners to speak or read
English, ultimately swindling thousands of families out of their pat-
rimony. (To this day, land-grant issues are still winding their way
through New Mexico's courts.) For financial reasons, by the early
1880s members of the Baca family had sold a large portion of their
shares in Baca Location No. 1 to three parties: brothers James and
Joel Whitney, who attempted to wrest control of the Baca family's
remaining shares; Thomas Catron, one of the era's most notorious
land-shark lawyers; and Catron's client Mariano Otero, a land spec-
ulator and the patriarch of one of New Mexico's most prominent

families (Martin 2003). Through a series of legal shenanigans too complicated to explain here, but which involved gunfights, midnight escapes, shell companies, and any number of subterfuges—as well as an ethically questionable court case concerning Baca Location No. 1 whereby Thomas Catron represented the Otero family in their claims against the Whitney brothers, who were represented by Catron's former law partners—the entire 100,000-acre parcel ultimately came under the Otero family's control (Martin 2003).

The Oteros continued to run sheep on the caldera, but they moved away from the traditional sharing of resources and instead leased grazing rights to local farmers. This was a system that bore more than a passing resemblance to medieval feudal systems and which ensured the Oteros turned a tidy profit. They also sought to exploit some of the area's natural resources, including mining for sulfur and pumice and developing the hot springs on the west side, which were seen as a potential tourist attraction. Additionally, Mariano Otero convinced the Santa Fe business community to help develop a proper road out of the wagon trail from Santa Fe to Valle Grande

Looking west across Valle Grande. Photo by Peter Dickson.

after offering to fund all but the last 2 miles himself (Martin 2003). However, by 1908 the Otero family was facing financial difficulty, in part due to disputes with community land-grant owners elsewhere, and they began looking for a buyer for Baca Location No. 1. In 1909, Redondo Development Company of Pennsylvania paid $300,000 (well over the market value of $53,000) for the land, with an eye to exploiting the vast forests that until then had been largely untouched (Martin 2003). However, without a nearby railroad and with passes blocked by snow the majority of the year, timber exploitation would have to wait. The Oteros continued to raise sheep on the land by leasing grazing rights from Redondo Development Company, running approximately 20,000 sheep and up to 3,000 cattle every year, far more than the land could carry in the short, five-month growing season (Martin 2003). The Otero Cabin in the Cabin District dates to 1915 and was built by the family as part of their grazing operation during this period.

In 1917 the Oteros decided not to renew their grazing lease, and brothers Frank and George Bond, who ran a mercantile business in Española, signed a five-year leasing contract with Redondo Development Company (Martin 2003). They built what are now known as the Bond Cabin and the Ranch Foreman's Cabin the next year, to serve as a summer home for their families and as a center of their ranching operations, respectively. They would later add the Commissary and the Old Barn in 1941, and the Red Office and the Greer Cabin in 1951. As a result of their inability to exploit the forests, Redondo Development Company became amenable to the Bond brothers' overtures to purchase the land outright. While they agreed to a sale in 1918, Redondo Development Company retained a ninety-nine-year lease on timber rights and 50 percent of mineral rights, effectively splitting ownership of Baca Location No. 1 and laying the foundation for decades of environmental degradation and legal disputes (Martin 2003). Despite this, the Bonds were pleased with their purchase and promptly established seventeen sheep camps, which were run by locals in a system similar to that of the Oteros. Under the Bonds' grazing system, herders had to manage their own sheep

The Old Barn and corral, built in 1941.

plus all of the Bonds' stock, assumed most of the risk, and were required to purchase their supplies from the Bonds' stores (Martin 2003). Needless to say, when the season was over it was always the Bonds who came out ahead. Many of the dendroglyphs (carvings on trees) that may still be seen in the far reaches of the preserve were carved by shepherds from this era.

The 1930s saw an increasing shift toward cattle ranching, particularly after NM 4 was modernized by the Civilian Conservation Corps, and by the end of World War II the market for sheep had collapsed with the development of synthetic fabrics and an increased demand for beef. By the 1950s almost 12,000 head of cattle were grazed in the caldera—far more than was truly sustainable—and as sheep were phased out, their shepherds were replaced by hired cowboys (Martin 2003). During this era, San Antonio Cabin was built adjacent to a hot spring in the northwest corner of the caldera, where hired cowboys could stay while tending herds. The Bonds also built a small cabin just off of Rito de Los Indios Trail (97), which was reputedly used

"Trujillo" dendroglyph along Rito de los Indios Trail (97).

by the Bonds to access their ranching operations from Española via Forest Road 144.

By 1957 both Bond brothers, as well as Frank's son Franklin, who had managed the ranch's operations, were dead, and their surviving family members leased the land to brothers Sam and Bruce King, who ended sheep grazing permanently. The King brothers wanted to buy Baca Location No. 1 but couldn't afford to purchase all of it, and the Bond family refused to partition it (Martin 2003). When word got out in 1961 that the Bond family was interested in selling, there was a concerted push locally and nationally to buy the land for the public. (This was not a new idea; recognition of the extraordinary natural and cultural value of the Jemez Mountains had been acknowledged for years. In the early 1900s there had been a similar push to protect vast swaths of land, including the caldera. While that was not achieved at the time, it did succeed in establishing Bandelier National Monument in 1916.) Unfortunately, by the time various

Cowboys in search of wayward cattle along La Garita Summit Trail (103). Photo by Peter Dickson.

federal agencies stopped quarreling over jurisdiction of the future park, the Bonds had sold the land to Patrick Dunigan, an oilman from Texas, for $2.5 million (Martin 2003).

Dunigan was interested in diversifying the uses of the caldera, exploring everything from an exclusive recreational and hunting resort to geothermal power, in additional to running cattle in the summer months. As part of this diversification, the A-frames and "witch's hat" lodge at the eastern end of the Cabin District were built by Dunigan both for family and for rich hunters who paid $10,000 each (in 1960s money) to try to shoot a trophy elk. After intense local outcry over the rumored possibility of high-end condos in Valle Grande, Dunigan retreated from his resort plans and focused on cattle and geothermal exploration. The first exploratory well was drilled in 1963 at Sulfur Creek, and when that seemed promising he brought in experts from Union Oil for further exploration. Union

Oil partnered with Public Service Company of New Mexico (PNM) in the 1970s, constructing offices and laying the foundation for a geothermal power plant along Redondo Creek (155). However, a lack of commercially adequate steam pressure combined with public concern about water rights and Pueblo peoples' spiritual interests led to the abandonment of the project by the early 1980s (Martin 2003). Scientists from Los Alamos National Laboratory and the US Department of Energy pursued a few more wells in the name of research, but this too came to an end. Additionally, Dunigan allowed crews from Hollywood to film in the caldera—a practice that continues to this day—the first production being *Shoot Out* starring Gregory Peck. Dunigan also briefly toyed with the idea of raising racehorses in the caldera and built the horse barn on the eastern edge of Valle Grande,

Abandoned geothermal wellhead in Sulfur Canyon (139).

reasoning that the high elevation would improve their performance, similar to the training regimen of elite marathon runners.

Dunigan was a conservationist in the tradition of Theodore Roosevelt, and he was interested in modern resource-management practices, particularly concerning the restoration of the valley grasslands that had been so damaged by overgrazing for nearly a century. He reduced cattle numbers to between 4,000 and 8,000 head, in part to help balance land use with the needs of the growing elk herd. What utterly appalled him, however, was the fact he could do nothing to stop Firesteel Lumber Company, which had bought the timber rights from Redondo Development Company in 1935, from ravaging his land. The construction of NM 4 in the 1930s made logging trucks practical for the first time, and by the time Dunigan bought Baca Location No. 1 from the Bond family, over 25,000 acres had been logged and miles of timber roads had been scraped into the hillsides (Martin 2003). Dunigan protested mightily, especially because the slash piles left behind drastically increased the fire danger, and the denuded hillsides suffered from erosion. From nearly the day he bought the land from the Bond family, Dunigan was in court against the timber company, suing for damages and to protect his interests. All the while, Firesteel Lumber continued to log as it pleased, ramping up production through such destructive practices as cable logging, whereby two trucks drive in parallel, a chain strung between them, and tear down any trees in their path. By 1971 there were over 1,000 miles of timber roads in the caldera, and the timber company was producing nearly 24 million board feet of lumber per year (Martin 2003). The remains of some of this era's sawmills may still be seen in some of the far reaches of the preserve. Finally, in 1972, after years of litigation and partial victories on both sides, Dunigan was able to buy the timber rights for $1.25 million and end commercial logging on his land (Martin 2003).

In 1975 Dunigan had Baca Location No. 1 designated as a National Natural Landmark, with the idea that the property could be preserved in perpetuity. This established a cooperative agreement with the National Park Service as part of a program to promote conservation of the nation's biological and geological resources. Dunigan did, however, sell two small sections. In 1975 he sold 165 acres on the eastern boundary to the Los Alamos Ski Club so that they could run their lift to the top of Pajarito Mountain. Two years later, he sold about 3,100 acres in the southeast corner of the property to Bandelier National Monument so that the Upper Frijoles Creek watershed could be part of one protected unit. In 1978 the National Park Service presented Dunigan with an attractive acquisition plan for the entire property, but bureaucratic infighting between agencies in Washington, DC, prevented the plan from proceeding (Martin 2003). In 1980, Dunigan died suddenly of a heart attack, and it seemed the opportunity to purchase the land for the public had been lost once again.

By this time, a wide variety of competing interest groups were in conflict over the future of the caldera: environmental groups, locals, Pueblo communities, outdoor enthusiasts, geothermal stakeholders, PNM, the US Forest Service, and others. Dunigan's heirs

Autumn colors in rejuvenating forest along Banco Bonito Loop (161).

insisted the land was not for sale, but in 1990 the Forest Service undertook a study of the property in the hope that someday it might be. In 1997, Dunigan's sons visited Washington, DC, to discuss the possibility with the Forest Service and with New Mexico's congressional delegation. Although Senator Jeff Bingaman (D) introduced legislation and the Clinton administration committed $20 million as a down payment, Senator Pete Domenici (R) was not convinced and was concerned about the financial viability of the potential park, as well as the already extensive federal land ownership in New Mexico. National interest in the caldera had grown, however, and many of the formerly competing interest groups banded together to voice their support for its purchase (Martin 2003). At one point a local woman even sat at a turnout overlooking Valle Grande along NM 4, urging passersby to sign a petition for public acquisition of the land.

A management model was developed out of a proposal initiated by the Cato Institute in Washington, DC, that would see Baca Location No. 1 governed by a board of nine trustees, five of whom were required to live in New Mexico, and that insisted on financial self-sufficiency within fifteen years. Domenici eventually got on board with the idea, hoping grazing and logging permits would pay the bills, but ultimately Bingaman was able to insert language into the enacting legislation that required the trust to follow all environmental laws. Negotiations between the Dunigan family and the federal government faltered several times over the next few years, but finally the bill to purchase the caldera was passed by the Senate, with the House agreeing on July 12, 2000, to a purchase price of $101 million dollars (Martin 2003). For about $1,000 per acre, Baca Location No. 1 was public land at last.

As part of the enacting legislation of what was now known as Valles Caldera National Trust, the governing board was required to preserve the multiuse history of the land, including cattle grazing, hunting, and fishing. Additionally, the trust was expected to work with local governments, including Pueblo communities. As part of this requirement, about 5,000 acres in the northeast corner of the

View of Valle Grande from the entrance to Hidden Valley (see Short Hikes, 40).

preserve was ceded to Santa Clara Pueblo, and it was agreed that no recreational activity would be allowed on or near sacred Redondo Peak (Martin 2003). This, along with Dunigan's earlier sale of land to the Los Alamos Ski Club and Bandelier National Monument, reduced the size of the property to about 89,000 acres. However, full public access was very slow in coming, which led to increasingly vocal public frustration, particularly among hikers, bikers, fishermen, and hunters. The public was finally granted limited access in August 2002, although the trust continued to struggle to balance public demand for access with protecting cultural sites, restoring damaged ecosystems, improving roads and other infrastructure, managing grazing, and limited financial revenues.

Due to its remote location in a sparsely populated state, and the challenges inherent in having a board split between locals and appointees who had limited understanding of New Mexico, the goal of self-sufficiency was never very likely to be met. As the fifteen-year deadline drew near, this was increasingly acknowledged to be the case, and a proposal to dissolve the trust and bring the caldera under the management of the National Park Service (NPS) was spearheaded by Caldera Action, a citizens' group, and the New Mexico Wildlife Federation, a hunters' and fishermen's group. The belief was that NPS could best protect the land, and that the New Mexico Department of Game and Fish could best manage hunting and grazing. Not everyone was thrilled by the idea—particularly ranchers, who were concerned they would lose access to the land. Local Pueblo communities also raised objections tied to their ancestral claims to the land amid concerns that they would lose ritual access to the caldera's resources. Senator Tom Udall (D) insisted on preserving grazing access, and Senator Martin Heinrich (D) succeeded in bringing the bill to a vote. The congressional designation that authorized the transition preserved previously granted access and promised to improve all public access, as well as ensure a steadier funding stream for much-needed work within Valles Caldera.

On December 19, 2014, Valles Caldera National Preserve became a unit of the National Park System. Since then public access has slowly improved, and the preserve leadership issued its Foundation Document in 2018, outlining plans for natural and cultural resource management, improved infrastructure, managed activities and uses, and wildland restoration (NPS 2018). Much work remains to be done, but the most important fact is that this treasure belongs to all of us now.

Sources for Further Reading

Anschuetz, Kurt F., and Thomas Merlan. 2007. *More than a Scenic Mountain Landscape: Valles Caldera National Preserve Land Use History*. Fort Collins, CO: US Department of Agriculture, Forest Service, Rocky Mountain Research Station.

Goff, Fraser. 2009. *Valles Caldera: A Geologic History*. Albuquerque: University of New Mexico Press.

Martin, Craig. 2003. *Valle Grande: A History of the Baca Location No. 1*. All Seasons Publishing.

NPS. 2018. *Foundation Document: Valles Caldera National Preserve, New Mexico*. Lakewood, CO: US Department of Interior, National Park Service, Intermountain Region.

Using This Guide

The trails in this guide are divided into two categories: short hikes, which are less than 3.5 miles long (round trip), and long hikes, which may be as much as 21 miles long (round trip). The short hikes are listed first, starting at the eastern boundary of the preserve along NM 4 and heading north into the preserve along the entrance road. These have brief descriptions of routes and conditions. The long hikes, which make up the majority of the trails, are listed second, starting with Coyote Call & Rabbit Ridge Trails (47) along NM 4 and proceeding into the backcountry largely counterclockwise. These have more detailed descriptions of routes and conditions, as well as maps. Apart from Coyote Call & Rabbit Ridge Trails and the last four long hikes, all long hikes require a backcountry vehicle permit to access the trailheads.

Each long hike is introduced by a trail map, essential information, and a brief list of trail conditions, followed by detailed instructions regarding the route. Be sure to review all of this information carefully before deciding on a trail to ensure it matches your abilities. For trails that require a backcountry vehicle permit, it is important to factor in the amount of time it takes to drive from the Entrance Station to the trailhead and return before the preserve closes for the day. Roughly speaking, from the Entrance Station it takes 25 minutes of driving time to reach Valle Jaramillo, 45 minutes to reach the T-junction, and about 1 hour to reach either end of the east–west backcountry access road. See the Accessing Valles Caldera National Preserve map (2), Regulations (32), and trail descriptions for more details.

Maps: Each long hike is described alongside a map indicating the direction and length of the trail. All maps use the UTM datum WGS84, Zone 13S. Coordinates for both UTM and degrees-minutes-seconds are included in the trail description. The contour interval on all maps is 40 feet. Note that scale varies considerably between each map.

- A trail route is indicated by a dashed line; where present, an alternative route is indicated by a solid line
- A trailhead is indicated by ⓉⒽ
- Trail names and/or numbers are indicated by 🖈 VC07
- Trail names and/or numbers specific to bikers are indicated by 🚲 VC03 (see Routes for Mountain Bikers, 168)
- A junction requiring a change of trail is indicated by •
- A trail terminus is indicated by ○
- A road open to vehicle traffic is indicated by ◇ VC02
- A locked iron gate is indicated by ✎
- Irrelevant or closed trails or timber roads are not indicated
- Locked cable gates that may be walked or biked around, or open gates, are not indicated

The maps included here are meant for informational purposes only. Hikers and bikers should always carry a map of the area where they are going, as well as a compass and/or a GPS, and know how to use them.

Currently there is no single, comprehensive map that reflects either all of the preserve's trails (either official trails or disused timber roads) or the reality on the ground. The routes in this guidebook were produced using Gaia GPS for iOS, with Gaia Topo, US Forest Service 2016, and US Geological Survey Topo layers. In my experience, this combination of three layers has generally been the most accurate when using GPS. Avenza Maps offers "Valles Caldera Trails" in its app, and while it is not nearly as comprehensive as the Gaia app, it does include the old road and trail numbers (e.g., VC03), which are helpful. Trail markings and signage are extremely poor in the preserve; hikers and bikers are strongly encouraged to use GPS for any of the trails.

For those who may want printed maps, the relevant US Forest Service 7.5 Minute Series Topographic Quadrangle maps are as follows: Redondo Peak Quadrangle, Bland Quadrangle, Valle San Antonio Quadrangle, Valle Toledo Quadrangle, Polvadera Peak Quadrangle, and Cerro del Grant Quadrangle. These are available for download at data.fs.usda.gov/geodata/rastergateway/states-regions/states.php. Or, contact your local US Forest Service office and ask if they carry hard copies.

Distance: All distances are round trip unless otherwise indicated. These are close approximations; actual distances may vary somewhat depending on the terrain.

Elevation Range and Gain: Elevation range indicates the lowest and highest points of the trail. Elevation gain indicates the approximate total number of feet ascended over the course of the hike; as a trail may go up and down, gain is not the same as the difference between the lowest and highest points. Hikers and bikers should take note that all of the trails in the preserve are well over 7,000 feet above sea level, and visitors are encouraged to acclimatize adequately before attempting any of the routes.

Difficulty: I follow the Northern New Mexico Group of the Sierra Club's trail-rating guidelines. An easy hike is generally 6 miles or less, with less than 1,000 feet of elevation gain. A moderate hike is generally 6–10 miles long, with 1,000–2,000 feet of elevation gain. A strenuous hike is generally longer than 10 miles, with more than 2,000 feet of elevation gain. There are some exceptions; for example, Cerro del Medio Loop (71) is nearly 14 miles long but has relatively little elevation gain and is therefore rated "moderate to strenuous." Note that the difficulty rating is based on a hiker's experience; where possible, I have added relevant information for bikers.

Recommended for Mountain Bikers: Unfortunately, due to the many destructive wildfires the preserve has suffered in the last decade, many trails are currently impassable to bikers. However, every year trail crews work to clear deadfall and improve access. I have noted whether trails are currently free (or mostly free) of deadfall and whether impassable trails will be good for bikers once they have been cleared. Trail conditions can change rapidly, however, so always check with the park rangers for the most up-to-date information before heading out on a ride.

See also the Routes for Mountain Bikers section (168) for longer routes suited to biking. While the preserve lacks single-track bike trails, many pleasant and challenging routes can be had by riding the largely vehicle-free backcountry jeep roads. Although no trails require advanced technical skills, conditions can be variable, and loose, rocky sections are common.

Conditions: This is a brief passage summarizing each trail, including recommended hiking direction, specific challenges, signage and navigation information, potential dangers or threats, sun and/or shade, ground conditions, and unique aspects of a given trail.

Trailhead: This includes details on where to park your vehicle and access the trail, followed by both degrees-minutes-seconds and UTM (datum WGS84, Zone 13S) coordinates.

Hike Details: This section elaborates on the details described in the Conditions section and provides an in-depth description of each trail, paying special attention to key junctions and tricky navigation, dangerous or challenging sections, and trail highlights. Read this section carefully for a thorough sense of the trail before heading out on your hike or ride. Note that the trail descriptions in this guide were as accurate as possible at the time of writing, but they are not a substitute for on-the-ground decisions and cannot predict changing trail conditions.

Regulations

Valles Caldera National Preserve is part of the National Park System, and therefore it has specific regulations that may be different from other public lands. Check the preserve website for the most up-to-date information: www.nps.gov/vall or call the VCNP information line at 575-829-4100. This list is not intended to be comprehensive, and regulations may change at any time without notice. It is your responsibility to know and follow all regulations while visiting the preserve.

The preserve is a fee park, although at the time of writing entrance fees were temporarily suspended. National Parks passes such as the Annual Pass are valid when entrance fees are charged. This entrance fee currently does not apply if accessing trails directly from NM 4 or Forest Road 105.

Any trails accessed via the backcountry access roads require a backcountry vehicle permit. This is free and is issued by park rangers at the Valle Grande Entrance Station. Permits are limited and are issued on a first-come, first-serve basis. It is strongly recommended to arrive early in the day, especially on weekends, in order to guarantee a permit. It is not possible to reserve a permit ahead of time. The backcountry access roads are rough but do not require four-wheel drive. Vehicles must stick to designated roads and park only in designated areas without blocking access to gates or fire roads.

The preserve is day-use only at this time. The US Forest Service operates several campgrounds along NM 4, as does nearby Bandelier National Monument. Lodging may also be found in Los Alamos, La Cueva, and Jemez Springs.

Summer season runs from May 15 to October 31. Summer hours are 8:00 a.m. to 6:00 p.m. The backcountry access roads are generally only open to private vehicles during the summer (conditions permitting), and all vehicles must check out with Entrance Station staff before the preserve closes for the day. Trails accessible from NM 4 and Forest Road 105 currently do not require a backcountry vehicle permit.

Winter season runs from November 1 to May 14. Winter hours are 9:00 a.m. to 5:00 p.m. Unless conditions permit, the backcountry access roads are generally not open to private vehicles during this period. It is possible to hike, bike, ski, or snowshoe from the Entrance Station into the backcountry, but distances are significant. All visitors must check out with Entrance Station staff before the preserve closes for the day. Trails accessible from NM 4 and Forest Road 105 may be hiked, biked, skied, or snowshoed in the winter season, but note that these are not maintained in any way during the winter.

Apart from Valle Grande (40), Coyote Call & Rabbit Ridge (47), and La Jara Trails (44), dogs are not allowed in the backcountry unless they are service animals. This prohibition includes within personal vehicles.

Smoking is only permitted inside personal vehicles. All smoking materials should be extinguished inside vehicles, never on the ground. Any fire restrictions in place at the time of your hike or ride apply.

Disturbing, collecting, or removing anything from the preserve—animals, plants, or minerals; antler sheds or obsidian; or artifacts or archaeological sites—is prohibited and is a federal offense.

Fishing is allowed within the preserve along East Fork of the Jemez River (including Hidden Valley), Jaramillo Creek, and San Antonio Creek. A New Mexico fishing license is required and must be presented on request. Check with the park rangers at the Entrance Station for the most up-to-date regulations.

Hunting is allowed within the preserve and is regulated by the New Mexico Department of Game and Fish (NMDGF). Turkey hunts occur in April and elk hunts occur from September to December. To apply for a hunting lottery, visit NMDGF's website: www.wildlife.state.nm.us/hunting. The hunting unit for VCNP is 6B. It is against the law to interfere with lawful hunters. Check with the park rangers at the Entrance Station for current information during hunting season.

Safety

While it does not take much to be adequately prepared and safe in the backcountry, similarly, it does not take much to make a mistake with potentially serious consequences. Ultimately, safety is your responsibility. Here are some basic safety rules every responsible hiker and biker should follow to avoid potential injury or even death.

Hike or bike with friends. Enjoy the backcountry in small groups, and tell someone where you are going and when you expect to return. Every year people are injured and sometimes die in the backcountry because they had no one to go for help, or no one knew where they were until it was too late.

Check in with park rangers. In addition to issuing you a backcountry vehicle permit, the rangers can offer up-to-date information on trail and weather conditions. Even if your trail does not require a vehicle permit, it's a good idea to talk with the rangers before heading out on your hike or ride.

Do not assume your cell phone will work. Many sections of the preserve lack cell coverage. Have a plan for accessing emergency assistance if something goes wrong. If you do have service, for medical emergencies call 911. For non-emergencies call 575-829-4100 (8:00 a.m. to 6:00 p.m.).

Plan your route ahead of time. Carry a GPS, a compass, and/or maps and know how to use them. Trail signage in the backcountry is very poor, a multitude of timber roads can make routes confusing, and it is extremely easy to get lost. The trail descriptions in this guide were as accurate as possible at the time of writing, but they are not a substitute for on-the-ground decisions and cannot predict changing trail conditions.

Check the weather. Despite its reputation for blue skies and endless sunshine, the weather in New Mexico can change rapidly, especially during the summer. Thunderstorms, wind, and lightning are the greatest threats to outdoor enthusiasts in New Mexico, especially along ridgelines and in open valleys, posing the very real risks of hypothermia and electrocution. If clouds are building up, consider your surroundings and turn back and/or seek shelter if necessary. Avoid lone trees and rocks or caves or depressions, separate members of your party by at least 30 feet, and stand on your pack to insulate yourself from the ground, crouching down with only your feet touching the ground.

Beware of loose rock and flash floods. Several trails within the preserve have sections with the potential for rockfall, as well as loose ground conditions that can cause injury. Additionally, several trails are near or pass through drainages or streambeds, which can flood without warning. Exercise caution when passing through any of these areas, and do not attempt to cross an arroyo if it is flowing.

Avoid burned areas. Many parts of the preserve have suffered from wildfire, including the massive 2011 Las Conchas and 2013 Thompson Ridge fires. As a result, trails often pass through areas of standing dead, burned trees, which pose a serious hazard in windy conditions. Do not linger in these areas when passing through, and do not enter in high winds.

Be prepared. Always carry the essentials in your pack: water, food, rain gear, GPS/compass/maps, sunscreen, hat, extra clothing layers, headlamp, whistle, pocketknife, and basic first aid. Consider what you would need if you were forced to spend a night without shelter, and pack accordingly. It is possible to die of exposure even in summertime. Wear boots that are well broken in and that offer arch and ankle support. Avoid cotton garments, as these take a dangerously long time to dry once wet; wear quick-dry synthetics instead.

Drink lots of water. The high elevations of the preserve and New Mexico's dry climate mean you will go through far more water than you may expect. If you are thirsty, you're already dehydrated. A good rule of thumb for staying hydrated is to always be on the edge of having to pee. In practice, this means at least 3 liters per day per person. There are very few water sources on the preserve, and what is present should be purified if you must drink it, so you should bring more than enough with you.

Take time to acclimatize. Altitude sickness can affect anyone, even if you are from the surrounding area. If you are from lower elevations, take a few days to adjust to the altitude in the area before attempting a trail. Drink lots of water, ascend slowly, and protect your skin with sunscreen. If you start to experience symptoms of altitude sickness, which include headache, nausea, dizziness, and fatigue, descend immediately to lower elevations.

Be alert to wildlife. The preserve is part of an enormous wildlife corridor in the Jemez Mountains, surrounded on all sides by acres and acres of protected lands. In addition to the thousands of elk for which it's famous, the preserve is home to black bears, mountain lions, mule deer, birds of prey, badgers, coyotes, pikas, prairie dogs, and many other birds, mammals, and reptiles. If you encounter an elk calf, leave it alone; its mother is nearby and is waiting for you to leave. Bear encounters are not uncommon, although it is extremely unlikely that you will encounter a mountain lion. In the event that you do encounter either animal, do not run. Raise your arms to appear as large as possible, make a lot of noise, throw stones or branches, and back away slowly, avoiding eye contact. Stand your ground if it charges, fight back, and if you are carrying bear spray, be prepared to use it.

Wilderness Ethics

The old adage of "take only pictures, leave only footprints" still applies. The principles below were developed by Leave No Trace and the Center for Outdoor Ethics and are the fundamental guidelines every outdoor enthusiast should follow. For more information, visit www.LNT.org.

The Leave No Trace Seven Principles

Plan ahead and prepare. As mentioned in Safety (35), having the right gear, including water, food, and first aid, as well as maps and a compass or GPS, is critical to a safe and enjoyable outing. Knowing how to use your gear, such as a GPS, is equally important. Before entering the backcountry, review the trail descriptions in this book, and check with park rangers for up-to-date conditions in order to find a trail that matches your skills and abilities. Be sure to check the weather, and don't forget to tell someone where you're going.

Travel and camp on durable surfaces. The preserve has suffered from many types of environmental degradation, both human-made and natural. It is important to stick to designated trails, avoid short-cuts between switchbacks or around muddy patches, and not wander through burned areas that are beginning to regenerate. Camping is not allowed in the preserve.

Dispose of waste properly. This is simple: if you pack it in, pack it out. This includes toilet paper. To dispose of solid waste properly, dig a cat hole at least 200 feet from a water source or trails, 6–8 inches deep and 4–6 inches wide, in an inconspicuous site away from where people are likely to travel (such as downed trees or thick under-growth). When finished, cover up the hole and disguise it with natural materials. If you find trash on the trail, be a good trail steward and pack it out.

Leave what you find. While this is always a good principle to follow, in the preserve it is a legal requirement. As noted in Regulations (32), disturbing, collecting, or removing anything from the preserve—animals, plants, or minerals; antler sheds or obsidian; or artifacts or archaeological sites—is prohibited and is a federal offense.

Minimize campfire impacts. Campfires are not allowed in the preserve. If you've planned correctly for your outing, lighting a fire to attract attention if lost or injured should never be necessary—more than one catastrophic wildfire has started this way.

Respect wildlife. You are very likely to encounter wildlife in the preserve, so it is important to give them space, avoid loud noises or quick movements (except regarding bears and mountain lions—see Safety, 35), and do not attempt to approach, touch, or feed them. A selfie with a bear is just not a good idea, and it can be extremely dangerous. If you find an elk calf alone, do not disturb it; its mother is nearby and is waiting for you to leave. Do not approach a sick or wounded animal; make note of its location, and notify the rangers before you leave. Remember that you are visiting the animals' home, and behave accordingly.

Be considerate of other visitors. Many people explore the backcountry to experience a feeling of solitude and connection with nature. Remember that an "outdoor voice" is actually a soft and quiet voice, and consider using earbuds if you wish to listen to music while hiking or biking. Uphill travelers have the right of way, and bikers should yield to hikers at all times regardless of the direction they're traveling. Additionally, the preserve is considered sacred by many of the Native American peoples of the Southwest, so bear that in mind and be a respectful visitor.

Short Hikes

At less than 3.5 miles round trip each, any of these trails are good for an easy, short introduction to the varied landscape of Valles Caldera National Preserve. Elevation gain is minimal. None require a backcountry vehicle permit. These are mostly unsuitable for mountain biking.

Valle Grande Trail

A 2-mile out-and-back trail that drops down the southern rim of the caldera to reach the southeastern side of Valle Grande. Dogs are permitted on this trail. Opportunities for elk sightings abound, both on the trail and out in the valley, especially early in the day or in the late afternoon and early evening. Access the trailhead near mile marker 43 on the north side of NM 4, opposite a parking area. The trailhead is marked with a signpost and a stile. The trail is clear and easy to follow, fading out as it reaches its terminus at a signpost on the valley floor. Retrace your steps to return the way you came. Note that the return is uphill.

Missing Cabin Trail

A 0.5-mile out-and-back trail that brings you to the Missing Cabin, so called because the set featured prominently in the movie *The Missing* (2003), parts of which were filmed in Valle Grande. The cabin is nestled in a picturesque setting, with good views toward Hidden Valley and across Valle Grande. Access the trailhead from the preserve

Terminus of Valle Grande Trail.

The Missing Cabin in Valle Grande.

Hidden Valley.

entrance road (VC01). The trail begins on the west side of the road about half a mile from the entrance off NM 4. Park near but do not block the locked cable gate. The trail is a clear dirt track up a short hill to reach the cabin. The cabin is unsafe to enter but is very photogenic. Retrace your steps to return the way you came.

Hidden Valley Trail

A 3.4-mile out-and-back trail that takes you along the lovely East Fork of the Jemez River as it flows westward into a narrow valley with fascinating volcanic formations and good opportunities for

View of Cerro La Jara from the entrance road.

wildlife and wildflowers. The trailhead and trail are informal and unmarked. Access the trail from the Missing Cabin trailhead, heading slightly north past the cabin and downhill toward the river, following the line of single trees. Once you reach the valley floor, turn left (southwest) and hike along the valley. Keep the river on your right until about 1.1 miles, where you will need to cross it using stepping-stones. At certain times of year these may be submerged. Continue following the river, now on your left, until the river leaves the preserve at the southern boundary fence line. In some areas close to the river the ground may be very marshy. Retrace your steps to return the way you came. Note that the return is uphill.

Ice on the pond in early spring.

La Jara Loop

A 1.5-mile loop that circles Cerro La Jara lava dome and offers everything from views of Valle Grande and the backcountry to volcanic
formations, wildflowers, elk, coyotes, badgers, and prairie dogs. Dogs
are permitted on this trail. Ask the rangers to lend you a trail guide.
Access the trailhead from the Valle Grande Entrance Station parking
area. The trail begins on the west side of the parking area and is
marked with a large brown sign and interpretive markers. The trail is
clear and easy to follow and is largely flat. Portions of the trail pass
through a prairie dog colony, so beware of open burrows.

Pond Trail

A 1-mile out-and-back trail that enters the heart of Valle Grande and terminates at a stock pond, with good opportunities for wildlife, waterfowl, and wildflowers. This trail should not be attempted when thunderstorms are threatening. Ask the rangers to lend you a trail guide. Access the trailhead from the Valle Grande Entrance Station parking area. The trail begins on the east side of the parking area and the south side of the livestock corral and is marked with brown posts. The trail is clear and easy to follow and is largely flat. After reaching the pond, retrace your steps to return the way you came.

Coyote Call & Rabbit Ridge Trails

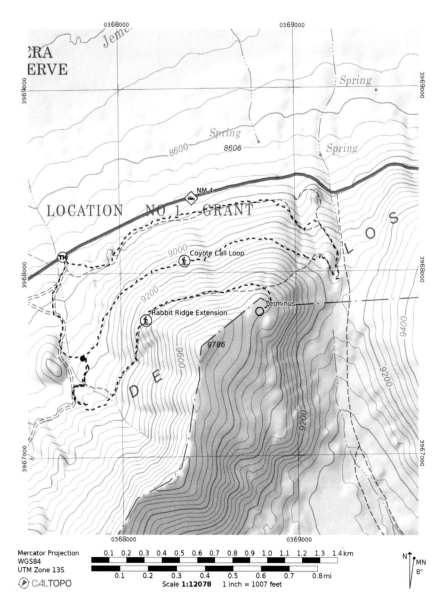

Coyote Call & Rabbit Ridge Trails

Two easy, linked trails with surprisingly good elevation gain, contouring up the side of Rabbit Mountain along the southeastern rim of the caldera and offering excellent views down into Valle Grande.

Distance (RT): 2.9 miles (Coyote Call Loop); 5.3 miles (with Rabbit Ridge Extension)

Elevation Range: 8,714–9,610 feet

Elevation Gain: 648 feet ascent (Coyote Call Loop); 1,701 feet ascent (with Rabbit Ridge Extension)

Difficulty: Easy

Recommended for Mountain Bikers: Yes for Coyote Call Loop, with potential for deadfall. Yes for Rabbit Ridge Extension, once deadfall is cleared.

Conditions: Coyote Call Loop may be hiked or biked in either direction; the out-and-back Rabbit Ridge Extension is steeper, and some hikers may prefer to do that first and end with the Loop. Rabbit Ridge dead-ends in a pile of deadfall at the boundary with Bandelier National Monument, and apart from additional distance and elevation it does not offer much more than Coyote Call on its own. A variety of trail markers are present, including trust-era wooden trailhead markers, blue blazes, yellow wooden posts, and brown posts—the combination of these can be a little confusing. The trail is generally in good condition and easy to follow, though in some places it can be a bit faint when wet years yield thick undergrowth. Standing dead trees along the trail pose a threat in high winds. It will be some years before the trail, once cleared, will remain clear, especially Rabbit Ridge. This trail should not be attempted when thunderstorms are threatening. Alternating sun and shade. Ground conditions may be grassy, gravelly, or rocky. Excellent opportunities for wildlife and wildflowers. Dogs are permitted on this trail. Collection of plants, antler sheds, obsidian, or other items is prohibited.

Trailhead: At the small pullout near mile marker 41 on the south side of NM 4.

Coordinates: 35° 50' 53.36" N, 106° 27' 55.11" W

UTM: 13S 367678 3968098

Hike Details

The trailhead is located on the south side of NM 4 and is marked with a gate, sign, and stile. Parking is available on either side of the highway (do not block the gates). Just past the stile is a Y-junction with a brown post on the left and a yellow wooden signpost on the right. Go left (east) to hike Coyote Call Loop first, as here, or right (southwest) to hike Rabbit Ridge Extension first. Heading east for Coyote Call Loop, the trail is slightly gravelly and climbs gently. Shortly after the Y-junction, the trail enters a small aspen grove with blue blazes on both sides of the trees. Very quickly views of Valle Grande emerge, each more impressive than the last as you slowly gain elevation. The trail alternates between treed areas and burned areas, and in wet years the first mile yields a tremendous variety of wildflowers.

After about 0.9 miles the trail begins a steady ascent, gently switchbacking up the hillside, again alternating between treed and burned areas. At about 1.2 miles the trees open out and the trail becomes steeper, and soon it takes a sharp right (northwest). This turn is poorly marked by felled trees on the ground, and the trail can be difficult to discern with thick undergrowth.

By 1.4 miles the trail is heading west and enters a dense aspen

Approaching the junction with Rabbit Ridge Extension.

grove on the edge of the burned area, and from here there are several downed trees blocking the trail that will require bikers to dismount. As the trees open out again, Redondito Peak comes into view on the horizon.

From 2 miles numerous game trails may be seen, as well as small pieces of obsidian scattered along the trail. The trail then passes through one more section of threatening standing dead trees before entering a pretty glade lined by aspen. At the far edge of the glade, at about 2.5 miles, is the junction with Rabbit Ridge Extension, marked by a damaged trust-era wooden trail marker and blue blazes on trees. Turn right (north) to return to the trailhead at NM 4; turn left (south) to hike the extension.

Immediately after joining Rabbit Ridge Extension, the trail begins

Peering down at Valle Grande from Rabbit Ridge Extension.

to ascend the hillside, switchbacking somewhat steeply up the mountain before heading east. The trail is generally easy to discern, although a few unmarked timber roads veer off the main trail in this section and may cause some confusion. As the trail ascends it again passes through burned areas, but in the initial section at least the standing dead trees pose less of a threat.

Just shy of 3 miles the trail becomes a bit steeper as it passes briefly through a grove before entering a burned area, but the climb is rewarded with wooden benches along the north side of the trail on which to sit and enjoy the fine views of Valle Grande and Redondo Mountain. After the benches the trail becomes considerably rockier and crosses a couple of drainages before entering an aspen grove.

From 3.5 miles the deadfall blocking the trail increases significantly, making it impassable to bikers. The trail begins to trend south at 3.6 miles and reaches the boundary between the preserve and Bandelier National Monument at 3.7 miles. This is marked by a Bandelier backcountry sign and wooden benches; any continuing trail into the monument is no longer maintained and is impassable at this point.

Retrace your route back to the junction with Coyote Call Loop, reaching it at 4.9 miles. Turn left (north and downhill), passing through another pretty meadow and a small grove of trees on your way, to return to the trailhead at NM 4 at 5.3 miles.

South Mountain Trail

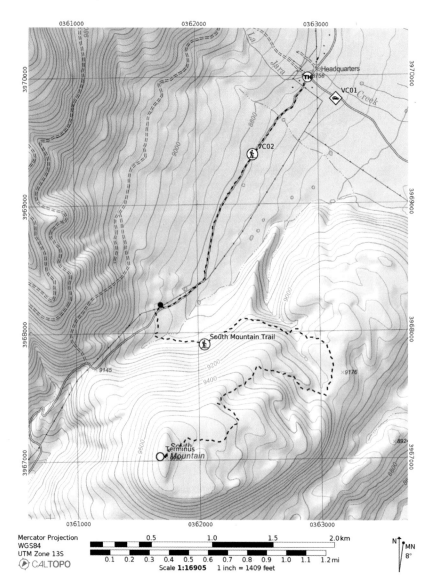

South Mountain Trail

A moderately challenging out-and-back hike up a forested hillside, reaching a pleasant meadow where the trail fades out before arriving at the summit, which offers great views eastward across the caldera.

Distance (RT): 8.2 miles
Elevation Range: 8,737–9,795 feet
Elevation Gain: 1,556 feet ascent
Difficulty: Moderate
Recommended for Mountain Bikers: Yes until the meadow, but the first half is entirely uphill and very aerobically challenging.
Conditions: The trail is hiked or biked as an out-and-back, with a sustained climb on the ascent. The formal trail does not extend to the actual summit and can be challenging to find on the return. From the meadow to the summit the trail is informal, and many hummocks and high grasses make for challenging walking. There are some trust-era yellow wooden signposts and some brown posts, and the trail is mostly easy to follow. After the jeep road ends there are blue blazes on trees, but these are a little difficult to see and the trail can be faint on the ground. The burned area near the summit has threatening standing dead trees, which should be avoided in high winds. This trail should not be attempted when thunderstorms are threatening. The trail is heavily forested and largely north facing, so there is good shade in summer and long-lasting snow well into spring,

except for the high meadow and summit. Ground conditions are gravelly or grassy.

Trailhead: At the locked cable gate marked VC02, in front of the Valle Grande Contact Station.

Coordinates: 35° 51' 51.93" N, 106° 31' 6.22" W

UTM: 13S 362912 3969976

Hike Details

From the Entrance Station, take VC01 (the backcountry access road) 1.7 miles to the Valle Grande Contact Station. There is parking adjacent to the Contact Station. The trail begins at the locked cable gate marked VC02 in front of the Contact Station; hike or bike along this gently rolling jeep road southwest up the valley behind South Mountain lava dome. After a little less than 1.5 miles, find the marked junction for South Mountain Trail on your left (south), just past the junction with VC0201 (see Redondo & Solitario Loops, 65). The trail enters a dense stand of ponderosa and Douglas fir, and within 0.2 miles it begins to switchback up the mountain. After about 2 miles the trail passes through a pretty aspen grove with views of Cerros del Abrigo and Valle Grande to the left (northeast). From 2.5 miles the incline increases as the trail climbs steadily, offering a few stretches of more level ground as respite but generally ascending for another mile.

At about 3.4 miles the jeep road ends and the trail continues straight (southwest) into a grove of aspen, climbing still more steadily with more switchbacks and trending southwestward. The trail is marked with blue blazes on trees, but these can be difficult to observe, and the trail can be quite faint on the ground. After another tenth of a mile the trail turns right (south) and contours briefly before returning southwest as it approaches the meadow.

At about 3.7 miles, the trail enters a lovely high meadow, which quickly opens out. Most of the trees surrounding the meadow and near the actual summit have suffered from fire damage and should be avoided in high winds. If continuing farther to the summit, make

View through aspens to Cerros del Abrigo (77) and beyond.

View of eastern Valle Grande from South Mountain summit.

note of where the trail enters the meadow as it can be difficult to spot on your return. From here to the summit the trail cannot be biked due to large and difficult hummocks. Head straight (southwest) across the meadow, aiming for a small aspen grove at the base of a small hill directly in front of you, reaching the trees at about 4 miles. A quick, steep climb up the hill brings you to the summit, which is covered by a small grove of stunted ponderosa trees. A patch of rocks under a small tree just shy of the summit offers excellent views eastward and makes a nice picnic spot. Do not attempt the summit or linger in the open meadow if thunderstorms are threatening.

Return the way you came, regaining the trail at the edge of the meadow and heading back downhill. Turn right (northeast) onto VC02 when you reach the junction at about 6.7 miles, and follow it back to the trailhead, returning to the Valle Grande Contact Station at about 8.2 miles.

El Cajete Loop

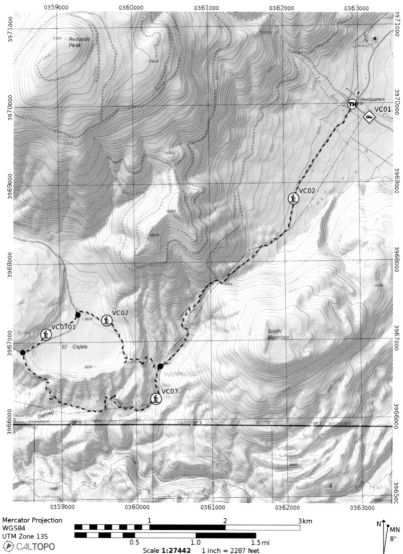

Mercator Projection
WGS84
UTM Zone 13S
CALTOPO

Scale **1:27442**   1 inch = 2287 feet

N↑ MN
8°

El Cajete Loop

A delightful and varied trail beginning at the Cabin District and passing through pretty meadows, groves of trees, and deposits of pumice and obsidian, reaching idyllic El Cajete Meadow at the halfway mark on the eastern edge of Banco Bonito lava flow.

Distance (RT): 9.4 miles
Elevation Range: 8,462–9,163 feet
Elevation Gain: 980 feet ascent
Difficulty: Moderate
Recommended for Mountain Bikers: Yes, with potential for deadfall. Washouts may require dismounting, and steep sections are aerobically challenging.
Conditions: The trail is best hiked or biked clockwise as described below, taking the VC07 leg of the loop on the way out and the VC02 leg on the way back to minimize steep sections. Four major washouts and a few steep sections add difficulty to an otherwise easy hike. Obsidian along the trail may pose a threat to bicycle tires. Note that this area is popular with bears, so be alert to the wildlife around you. Signage is minimal and mostly in the form of brown posts but is not difficult to follow. Standing dead trees along the trail pose a threat in high winds. Hikers and bikers should not linger at El Cajete Meadow, on ridgelines, or in the washouts when thunderstorms are threatening. Do not attempt to cross washouts when flowing or if rainstorms are in the area, as extremely dangerous flash floods can

occur without warning. Alternating sun and shade. Ground conditions may be rocky, sandy, or grassy. Sections of the trail contain large pieces of pumice and obsidian. Prairie dogs may be seen at the meadow. Good opportunities for wildlife and wildflowers. Collection of plants, antler sheds, obsidian, or other items is prohibited.

Trailhead: At the locked cable gate marked VC02, in front of the Valle Grande Contact Station.

Coordinates: 35° 51' 51.93" N, 106° 31' 6.22" W

UTM: 13S 362912 3969976

Hike Details

From the Entrance Station, take VC01 (the backcountry access road) 1.7 miles to the Valle Grande Contact Station. There is parking adjacent to the Contact Station. The trail begins at the locked cable gate marked VC02 in front of the Contact Station; hike or bike along this gently rolling jeep road southwest up the valley behind South Mountain lava dome. After a little less than 1.5 miles, pass the marked junction for South Mountain Trail (53), just past the junction with VC0201 (see Redondo & Solitario Loops, 65). Once you are past the junctions, the trail begins a steady, steep climb through patches of burned trees and occasional deadfall.

Just shy of 2 miles the trail tops out and offers fine views to the southwest. From here, obsidian may be spotted along the trail, with large specimens quite common. The trail then begins a long descent of about half a mile, passing through several burned areas with sections that may be hazardous in high winds. In the lower half of the descent, the trail suffers from significant erosion along its edges.

At 2.5 miles the trail finishes its descent, enters a small meadow, and crosses a rocky streambed. The trail becomes a little faint at this point, so proceed straight (southwest) to reach the first of the washouts at 2.6 miles. The washout is full of huge chunks of pumice and requires a scramble down to reach the other side. After proceeding down the washout the trail continues somewhat faintly, becoming

Looking east across El Cajete Meadow.

gravelly with loose small pebbles. At 2.8 miles the trail reaches the
second and worst of the washouts, requiring a scramble in and out.
This one would be extremely dangerous in the event of rain or flash
flooding.

Shortly after the second washout the trail reaches the Y-junction
of VC07 and VC02, marked by brown posts for each trail. Take VC07
(the left fork) and trend south, passing through another eroded
section and reaching the third major washout just after 3 miles. As
before, this requires a scramble in and out and would be extremely
dangerous in the event of rain or flash flooding. After exiting the
washout the trail becomes a pleasant, winding jeep road that is clear
and easy to follow. It climbs steadily and passes through several
pretty ponderosa groves, cresting at about 4 miles in a small glade.

At about 4.2 miles the trail resumes its climb, ascending more
steeply now, with views south as it nears its summit. At about 4.8 miles
the trail reaches its summit, and El Cajete Meadow may be seen
through the trees to your right (northeast). After a short distance the

Looking west across El Cajete Meadow.

trail reaches the junction with VC0701; turn right (northeast) onto VC0701 and head toward the meadow. Both trails are marked with brown posts, although these are not immediately visible from the junction. There is a small pond at the edge of the meadow and a few prairie dogs, as well as extensive elk sign, and in wet years you may hear peeper frogs chirping away. Skirt the edge of the meadow as you head northeast, passing a natural cave formed by a lava air pocket on your left (west) at about 5.1 miles.

Just shy of 5.5 miles the trail reaches a T-junction; turn right (southeast) onto VC02 and follow the trail as it enters a treed area and skirts the north side of El Cajete Meadow. This is marked with a brown post that is not immediately visible from the junction. The trail crosses a few dry, rocky washes and offers lovely views westward across the meadow. At about 6 miles the trail begins a moderately steep climb into stands of ponderosa, becoming a clear dirt track strewn with pine needles and occasional deadfall.

At 6.3 miles the trail takes a sharp left (northeast) and proceeds steeply downhill, reaching the fourth major washout at 6.4 miles and ending the loop by rejoining VC07 at 6.5 miles. Turn left (northeast) here for the final leg of the trail, retracing your path uphill. At about 7.5 miles the trail reaches the summit of the climb, and then it heads downhill back to the trailhead, returning to the Valle Grande Contact Station at 9.4 miles.

Redondo & Solitario Loops

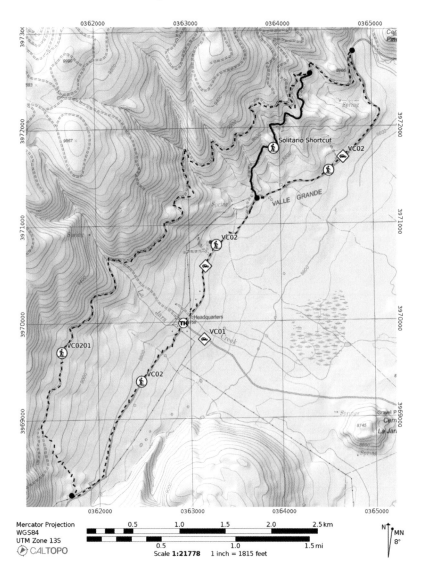

Mercator Projection
WGS84
UTM Zone 13S

Scale **1:21778**   1 inch = 1815 feet

Redondo & Solitario Loops

An easy loop trail with moderate elevation gain offering extensive views of Valle Grande, passing through both forested groves and burned areas, with two trail options on the return.

Distance (RT): 8.6 miles (with Solitario Shortcut); 9.6 miles (without Solitario Shortcut)

Elevation Range: 8,630–9,148 feet

Elevation Gain: 1,305 feet ascent (with Solitario Shortcut); 1,292 feet ascent (without Solitario Shortcut)

Difficulty: Easy to moderate

Recommended for Mountain Bikers: Yes for Redondo Loop, with potential for deadfall. Yes for Solitario Shortcut, once deadfall is cleared.

Conditions: The trail is best hiked or biked clockwise, as described below. Solitario Shortcut reduces the distance by approximately 1 mile. Elevation gain is minor and both options are otherwise not challenging. Signage is poor and infrequent; where present, it is generally brown or wooden posts. Deadfall was cleared over the summer of 2018, with the result that VC0201 is now in reasonably good condition, though still potentially problematic for mountain bikers. Many threatening standing dead trees remain, and it will be some years before the trail, once cleared, will remain clear. Caution is advised during high winds. Solitario Shortcut has not been cleared and is currently not suitable for mountain bikers. A few eroded and washed-out sections are present but are passable, although they may require bikers to dismount. Do not attempt to cross these washouts when flowing or if rainstorms are in the area, as extremely dangerous flash floods can occur without warning. The last stretch along VC02 is open to vehicle traffic. Mostly full sun all day. Ground conditions are mostly gravel, with some sections of grass or loose rock. Solitario Shortcut rejoins VC02 (the backcountry access road) next to cabins built for the movie *Shoot Out* (1971). Good opportunities for elk sightings along the many game trails.

Trailhead: At the locked cable gate marked VC02, in front of the Valle Grande Contact Station.

Coordinates: 35° 51' 51.93" N, 106° 31' 6.22" W

UTM: 13S 362912 3969976

Hike Details

From the Entrance Station, take VC01 (the backcountry access road) 1.7 miles to the Valle Grande Contact Station. There is parking adjacent to the Contact Station. The trail begins at the locked cable gate marked VC02 in front of the Contact Station; hike or bike along this gently rolling jeep road southwest up the valley behind South Mountain lava dome. After a little less than 1.5 miles, find the junction with VC0201 on the right (north), just before the marked junction with South Mountain Trail (53). The trail is marked by a brown post that is not immediately visible from VC02. The trail is initially a grassy track, nicely wooded with big ponderosa and Douglas fir, although from here to the eastern junction with VC02 (the backcountry access road) there is always the possibility of downed trees. About 0.2 miles after joining VC0201, the grassy track forks at an unmarked junction; take the left (northwest) fork. The trail then begins a moderate, steady climb for about half a mile. This is the majority of the elevation gain for the entire trail.

At just under two miles, the trail turns northeast and enters the fire-damaged area. Shortly thereafter, turn right (northeast) at the unmarked T-junction. From here the trail becomes a flat track, with the ascent effectively completed for the remainder of the trail, and it contours along the hillside for the next 4-plus miles. The burned areas are generally exposed and can be quite hot in the summer, as well as potentially dangerous in high winds due to the significant number of standing dead trees, but they do offer the advantage of nice views of Valle Grande along much of the trail.

In spring and in wet years there are some small streams and muddy seeps that cross the trail, but most of these are crossed without difficulty. There are two notable exceptions: at 3.5 miles the trail crosses La Jara Creek, and at 4.7 miles the trail crosses an unnamed drainage, both of which are washed out and require a bit of a scramble to cross. Mountain bikers may need to dismount at these crossings. These could be dangerous in the event of rain or flash flooding.

After about 5 miles the forest improves, offering some welcome shade, and the trail crosses a few shallow arroyos. At approximately 5.8 miles, VC0301 (Valle Jaramillo Loop, 83) joins the trail from the left (north); veer right (northeast) to remain on VC0201, trending downhill and into a burned area. Brown posts mark this junction.

Looking south across eastern Valle Grande.

The Solitario Shortcut junction is on the right (south) at just under 6.5 miles, marked with wooden signs for Solitario and History Grove. While Solitario Shortcut does not appear on VCNP official maps, the trail is easy to follow (see below). For the full loop, continue eastward, passing through pretty glades and enjoying clearer views of the eastern side of Valle Grande.

At approximately 7 miles, VC0201 ends at the junction with VC02 (the backcountry access road). Turn right (south) and follow the road back to the starting point, enjoying sweeping views of Valle Grande as you go. This section is open to vehicle traffic. Enter History Grove, one of the few remaining stands of old-growth ponderosa on the preserve, pass the lower junction with Solitario Shortcut at 8.6 miles, and continue on VC02 toward the Cabin District. In spring there are large fields of wild iris in the marshy areas between History Grove and the Cabin District. These cabins date to when the preserve was a privately held ranch, the majority of which are from the first half of the twentieth century. Return to the trailhead and the Valle Grande Contact station at 9.6 miles.

Last leg of Redondo Loop along VC02.

Solitario Shortcut

If you wish to shorten your hike by a mile, take Solitario Shortcut from VC0201 and follow the old trail as it slowly contours southwest around and down the hillside, being cautious as you scramble over the downed trees that litter the trail. There is so much deadfall that Solitario Shortcut is currently impassable to bikers. The trail is not marked, but the jeep road is very clearly defined. Much of Solitario Shortcut passes through burned areas, so caution is advised in high winds. At approximately 7.5 miles, the old movie-set cabins along VC02 (the backcountry access road) in History Grove will be visible in front of you; the trail here can be very faint, so aim in their direction. The trail rejoins VC02 just below the cabins. This section is open to vehicle traffic. Turn right (southwest) and follow the road back to the trailhead, returning to the Valle Grande Contact Station at 8.6 miles.

Cerro del Medio Loop

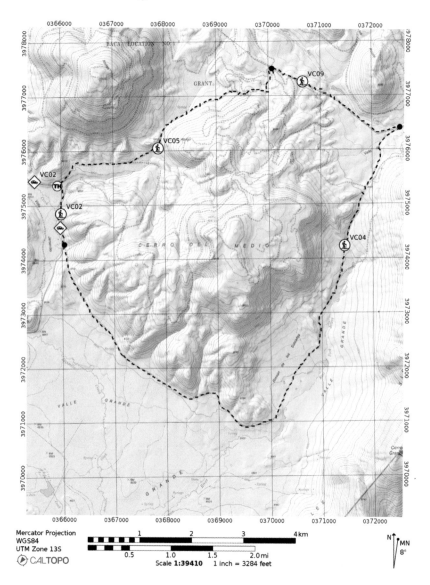

Mercator Projection
WGS84
UTM Zone 13S

CALTOPO

Scale **1:39410**   1 inch = 3284 feet

N
MN
8°

Cerro del Medio Loop

A gently rolling trail with minor elevation gain, passing through Obsidian Valley, forested groves, secluded backcountry valleys, and some burned areas, with great views of Valle Grande along the latter half of the trail.

Distance (RT): 13.8 miles
Elevation Range: 8,563–9,016 feet
Elevation Gain: 1,216 feet ascent
Difficulty: Moderate to strenuous
Recommended for Mountain Bikers: Yes, with potential for significant deadfall in a few sections.
Conditions: The trail may be hiked or biked in either direction; the description here is clockwise. Note that this area is popular with bears, so be alert to the wildlife around you. Obsidian along the trail may pose a threat to bicycle tires, especially over the first 3.5 miles along VC05. Lack of signage, numerous old timber roads, and the potential for significant deadfall mean GPS is essential. Near the junction of VC05 with VC09, the trail passes through a burned area with high potential for deadfall, and at times it can become exceptionally difficult to follow. Although this area was partially cleared in 2019, many threatening standing dead trees remain, and it will be some years before the trail will remain clear. Caution is advised during high winds. There are two sections, each several miles in length, where the trail crosses open meadows, which should not be entered

when thunderstorms are threatening. The last stretch along VC02 is open to vehicle traffic. Full sun all day, other than in occasional forested groves. Ground conditions are mostly gravelly or sandy. Good opportunities for wildlife sightings, especially in the autumn when the elk are in the rut. Huge specimens of obsidian may be seen along VC05. Collection of plants, antler sheds, obsidian, or other items is prohibited.

Trailhead: At the locked cable gate marked VC05, on the right (east) side of VC02 (the backcountry access road).

Coordinates: 35° 54' 48.95" N, 106° 29' 9.55" W

UTM: 13S 365921 3975385

Hike Details

From the Entrance Station, take VC01–VC02 (the backcountry access roads) for approximately 6.5 miles to Valle Jaramillo, and look for the locked cable gate marked VC05 on the right (east) side of the road. There is a small parking area at the trailhead (do not block the gate). From the trailhead, the trail begins as a very gently ascending jeep road, winding its way along the northern side of Cerro del Medio, through groves of ponderosa and Douglas fir and up Obsidian Valley. Large chunks of obsidian, some as large as boulders, may be seen along the trail for most of the next 4 miles.

After a gentle climb, at about 1.5 miles the trail enters a burned area along the northern side of Cerro del Medio, with the potential for deadfall across the trail increasing for the next 3 miles. Soon the trail skirts a peaceful meadow as it enters upper Obsidian Valley, with good views toward the northeastern rim of the caldera. At about 2 miles the trail suffers from significant erosion and may require bikers to dismount. From here to the junction with VC09, the standing dead forest poses a threat to hikers and bikers alike, and caution should be exercised during high winds. At the same time, this is an excellent area for elk sightings, especially in the autumn during the rut.

At about 2.6 miles the trail begins to climb gently, but it quickly becomes faint and can be lost entirely if deadfall obscures the track.

Upper Obsidian Valley.

For approximately the next mile, numerous old timber roads and a lack of signage, as well as old gates and seemingly conflicting markers, make finding the junction with VC09 very challenging. For example, at about 3.4 miles, VC0501 joins VC05, both of which are marked with brown posts, but VC0501 is not on current maps, and the junction is close enough to the correct junction at VC09 on GPS and similar enough on the ground that it is easy to be misled. Go left (north) here for VC05 (the marker is not immediately visible at the junction); shortly thereafter join VC09 and turn right (southeast). VC09 is marked with a brown post and is an obvious backcountry access jeep road, which follows a New Mexico Gas Company pipeline that serves the town of Los Alamos.

After joining VC09, deadfall is no longer an issue, and the trail is a gently rolling sandy track that passes through ponderosa groves and enters tranquil Valle de los Posos. At about 4.4 miles the trail passes a stock pond on the left (north) and the valley begins to open out,

Storm clouds gathering over Valle de los Posos. Photo by Peter Dickson.

reaching the junction with VC04 at about 5.4 miles. VC09 is marked with a brown post at this junction, but the marker for VC04 has fallen down. Mountain bikers who wish to exit the preserve via the eastern rim of the caldera should continue on VC09 to reach Cañada Bonita and Pajarito Mountain Ski Area (see Routes for Mountain Bikers, 168). To continue our loop, turn right (southwest) onto VC04 and head down the valley, keeping an eye on the weather if thunderstorms are threatening. Some sections of the trail may be muddy or rutted, but it is generally in good condition and easy to follow.

After about 6.5 miles the trail is less exposed and hugs the side of Cerro del Medio as it heads toward Rincon de los Soldados. Alternating stands of burned and live ponderosa, as well as several pretty, small glades, offer good opportunities for elk sightings. At about 7.75 miles Rincon de los Soldados opens out, offering views of

Passing through Rincon de los Soldados.

Valle Grande, but for the next 4 miles the trail is very exposed. The trail is slightly sandy and largely flat with a few gentle rolls, and at 9.6 miles it begins to curve northwest after passing an old jeep road (VC0401) on the left (south) that leads up to NM 4. Mountain bikers who wish to connect with NM 4 should do so here (see Routes for Mountain Bikers, 168).

Enjoying sweeping views of Valle Grande on your left (southwest), from about 10.5 miles the trail crosses several rocky washes, with healthy groves of young ponderosa on the west face of Cerro del Medio. The trail enters a stand of trees at about 12 miles, and 1 mile later VC04 ends at VC02 (the backcountry access road). Turn right (north) and follow the road, which is open to vehicle traffic, for just under 1 mile to return to the trailhead at 13.8 miles.

Cerros del Abrigo Loop

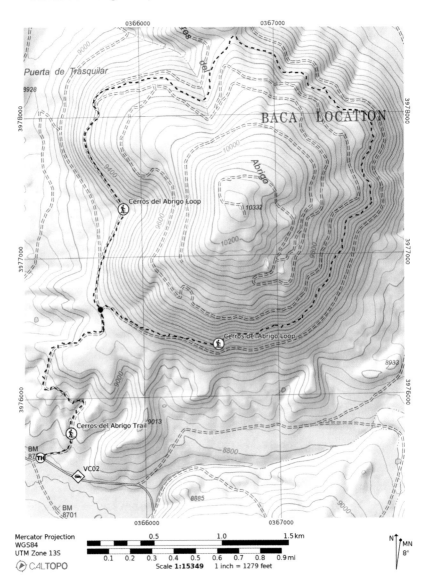

Scale **1:15349**   1 inch = 1279 feet

Cerros del Abrigo Loop

Despite the heavy damage Cerros del Abrigo have suffered due to logging and fire, this is a delightful trail that contours around a lava dome after the initial ascent, offering impressive views of many of the preserve's prettiest valleys.

Distance (RT): 7.2 miles
Elevation Range: 8,720–9,559 feet
Elevation Gain: 1,515 feet ascent
Difficulty: Easy to moderate
Recommended for Mountain Bikers: Yes, although ground conditions change rapidly.
Conditions: The trail may be hiked or biked in either direction around the lava dome, but as hiked (counterclockwise) most elevation gain is achieved early in the hike. Bikers may wish to travel clockwise for a gentler ascent. Deadfall was cleared over the summer of 2019, although stumps of aspen in the trail are just high enough to trip hikers or catch bike wheels, and the potential for future deadfall is significant. Note that this area is popular with bears, so be alert to the wildlife around you. Signage is generally good though occasionally confusing, with yellow wooden posts indicating direction counterclockwise (for the most part) and brown metal posts indicating direction clockwise (for the most part). Standing dead trees pose a threat in high winds, and most of the trail is exposed and should not be attempted when thunderstorms are threatening. Full sun all day. Ground conditions

change rapidly and may be gravelly, grassy, or rocky, and some sections will be tediously challenging for bikers. Many young aspen groves are beginning to dot the trail as the forest rejuvenates. Excellent opportunities for elk sightings and wildflowers.

Trailhead: At the locked cable gate marked VC0203, on the right (east) side of VC02 (the backcountry access road).

Coordinates: 35° 54′ 55.34″ N, 106° 29′ 37.81″ W

UTM: 13S 365216 3975593

Hike Details

From the Entrance Station, take VC01–VC02 (the backcountry access roads) for approximately 7 miles to Valle Jaramillo, and look for the locked cable gate marked VC0203 on the right (east) side of the road. There is also a small wooden sign marking the Cerros del Abrigo trailhead. There is a small parking area at the trailhead (do not block the gate). From the trailhead, the trail starts as a gentle uphill climb northeastward on a grassy track, passing a trust-era wooden trail marker and an outhouse. The trail then enters a burned area and begins to climb more steeply, curving around the hillside as it ascends. Within the first half mile you begin to have lovely views of the surrounding valleys, starting with Valle Jaramillo. In places along this stretch the edge of the trail can be quite eroded, but it is still wide enough to allow for easy passage.

After just over 1 mile, the trail enters a small grove of trees and then reaches the junction with the loop. Here you will a find brown post with arrows pointing straight (north) and right (east) for the loop trail, as well as a downed yellow wooden post nearby indicating the counterclockwise direction. Turn right (east) to travel around Abrigo counterclockwise, beginning with a gentle climb. Go straight (north) to travel around Abrigo clockwise. (Either direction is fine, but counterclockwise, as here, gains more elevation more quickly and is slightly easier to follow.)

Traveling counterclockwise from the junction, within the next

View of Valle Jaramillo and Valle Grande from Cerros del Abrigo Loop.

half mile there are several deep and rocky eroded gullies that will be challenging for bikers. At approximately 1.4 miles, an old timber road descends to the right; take the left trail that climbs gently, trending eastward. As you ascend, you will be rewarded with fine views of Valle Grande and Obsidian Valley. Keep your eye out for elk as this area is crisscrossed with game trails.

Near the 2-mile mark an old timber road comes down from above on your left (north); continue straight ahead as the trail flattens out and heads almost due east, with views of upper Obsidian Valley and the eastern rim of the caldera. The trail passes through alternating stands of young aspen and burned trees, with a few rocky sections that will be challenging for bikers. When passing through the stands of young aspen, be alert for low-lying stumps from cleared saplings in the middle of the trail, as these can catch bike wheels and trip hikers.

The trail begins to trend northward at about 3 miles, offering views of Valle de los Posos and again passing through alternating stands of young aspen and burned trees, with occasional rocky sections. As the trail continues northward, Valle Toledo and the northeastern rim of the caldera will come into view. This is one of the prettiest sections of the trail.

After 4 miles the trail takes a sharp left (southwest) and crosses an open saddle as it begins its return leg. There are old stumps blocking a disused timber road to the right (north) of the turn, as well as some minor signage. The saddle is very exposed, so caution is advised in threatening weather. As you cross the saddle, game trails and old timber roads can be misleading, so pay close attention to the trail and aim southwest. Around 4.2 miles an old timber road joins the trail from the left (east); do not take this uphill but rather continue straight ahead on the right (south). Shortly thereafter the trail crosses a talus field and passes through a burned area, with views of Cerros Santa Rosa and La Garita opening out as the trail trends downhill.

After 5 miles you will begin to see Valle Jaramillo and Redondo Peak to the southwest, and gradually Valle Grande as well. As before, old timber roads join the trail, but the main trail is obvious and

Talus field along the trail in early winter.

continues steadily downhill. (Hikers and bikers traveling clockwise will need to be more attentive to the correct trail, as signage is poor and confusing at times.) In another half mile a huge talus field crosses the trail, appearing as a wall as the trail passes beneath it and enters a shady stretch of trees.

On entering the burned area the trail becomes very uneven and rocky, with eroded gullies along the edges of the trail extending until the trail returns to the loop junction at about 6 miles. At the junction, turn right (south) to retrace the way you came and return to the trailhead at 7.2 miles.

Valle Jaramillo Loop

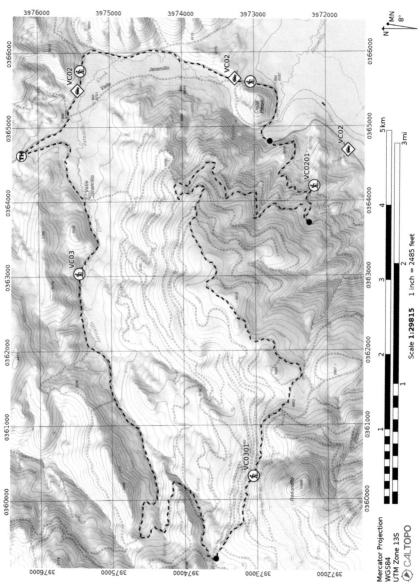

Valle Jaramillo Loop

A moderately challenging but lengthy trail along old jeep roads passing through pretty Valle Jaramillo and skirting the back of Redondo Mountain, with rewarding views of both the northern and southern rims of the caldera.

Distance (RT): 13.7 miles (with two-car shuttle); 17.1 miles (without two-car shuttle)

Elevation Range: 8,687–10,000 feet (with two-car shuttle); 8,595–10,000 feet (without two-car shuttle)

Elevation Gain: 2,000 feet ascent (with two-car shuttle); 2,114 feet ascent (without two-car shuttle)

Difficulty: Strenuous

Recommended for Mountain Bikers: Yes, once deadfall is cleared.

Conditions: The trail is best hiked or biked counterclockwise as described below, starting from VC03 and ending via VC0201. A two-car shuttle is strongly recommended to save an extra 3.4 miles along VC02 (the backcountry access road) at the end. The hike is challenging due to its length but ascents are gradual. Lack of signage makes navigation difficult in some areas due to extensive timber roads lending confusion to the route; GPS is strongly recommended. Where present, signage is brown posts. There is considerable deadfall blocking the trail beginning at the junction with VC0301 and continuing to VC0201, and standing dead trees pose a threat in high winds. This trail should not be attempted when thunderstorms are threatening. If not using a two-car shuttle, note that the last stretch along VC02 is open to vehicle traffic. Alternating sun and shade. Ground conditions may be gravelly, rocky, or muddy. Many game trails crisscross the trail, with elk sightings likely.

Trailhead: At the locked cable gate marked VC03 at the northern end of Valle Jaramillo, just before a cattle guard on VC02 (the backcountry access road), on the left (west) side of the road.

Coordinates: 35° 55' 14" N, 106° 30' 1.37" W

UTM: 13S 364634 3976177

If using a two-car shuttle, leave one car at the locked cable gate marked VC0201 on the left (west) side of VC02 (the backcountry access road) before proceeding to the VC03 trailhead.

Coordinates: 35° 53' 23.65" N, 106° 29' 52.56" W

UTM: 13S 364803 3972773

Hike Details

From the Entrance Station, take VC01–VC02 (the backcountry access roads) for approximately 4 miles to the locked cable gate marked VC0201 on the left (west) side of the road. If using a two-car shuttle, leave one car here (do not block the gate). Continue another 3.4 miles to Valle Jaramillo, and look for the locked cable gate marked VC03 on the left (west) side of the road. There is a small parking area at the trailhead (do not block the gate). The trail begins as a largely flat, gravelly jeep road that quickly turns west up Valle Jaramillo, with Jaramillo Creek on your left (south) and small groves of ponderosa along the edge of a burned area on your right (north). After about three-quarters of a mile, the trail crosses a cattle guard and the valley begins to narrow. The exclosures along the stream to your left (south) are part of scientific studies of the riparian ecosystem. At about 1 mile, the trail passes through an open iron gate and begins to ascend very gradually.

From 2 miles, in addition to occasional erosion along the trail, there is a small burned area along the right (north), with only a few threatening standing dead trees. After another half mile, the valley narrows considerably, with stands of ponderosa pines closing in on both sides of the trail.

Occasional deadfall and erosion continue to dot the trail until about 3.4 miles, when the trail enters a forested grove. The grove quickly gives way to another burned area with more deadfall blocking the trail, as well as threatening standing dead trees. At 3.8 miles the trail begins a steady climb up and around the western end of the valley, trending north and west. There is no signage here, and the deadfall can make the trail difficult to discern. At about 4.1 miles, as the trail continues to ascend, it curves left (southwest and then east) as it approaches the backside of Redondo Mountain on the opposite side of Valle Jaramillo from where you started.

From here there are burned areas on both sides of the trail, with occasional deadfall for the next half mile. Be cautious when passing through here in high winds. In another tenth of a mile the

Western end of Valle Jaramillo.

View of the north rim of the caldera.

trail levels out and begins to curve gently west, gaining elevation very slowly. There is more erosion along the trail here, but nothing impassable.

Just past 5 miles, an old timber road splits off to the left (south) and is cut by a small creek; the trail continues straight (west). At about 5.3 miles the trail reaches a second junction with a timber road and again continues straight. Neither of these junctions are marked, so pay close attention to your direction.

At 5.75 miles the trail reaches the junction with VC0301, which is marked by an open iron gate and a brown post. Mountain bikers who wish to connect with VC06 should turn right (north), or continue straight (west) to connect with Redondo Creek (see Routes for Mountain Bikers, 168). To continue our loop, turn right

Crossing the saddle with Valle Grande in the distance.

(southeast) onto VC0301 and begin a steady uphill climb. From about 6 miles the trail gradually levels out, offering views of the northern rim of the caldera as the trail continues southeastward. At about 6.4 miles the trail passes through a small aspen grove and across a talus field, but from here wildfire has eliminated the trees and the views north are unobstructed. At 7 miles on a clear day, you can even see as far as Truchas Peaks to the northeast.

At about 7.2 miles the trail reaches its highest point, at the junction of VC0301 and VC030101, which is marked by another open iron gate and brown posts. Stay on VC0301 and continue straight (east) and downhill. This section is very exposed and should be avoided when thunderstorms are threatening. From here until returning to VC02 (the backcountry access road), the chances of seeing elk are very good.

At about 7.3 miles the trail is very eroded as it crosses a heavily burned saddle, and deadfall across the trail increases considerably. Fortunately, the trail is obvious and easy to follow. At 7.6 miles there is a small stock pond on the right (south) side of the trail, and in another half mile Valle Grande may be seen to the south.

The burned area continues as the trail proceeds along the saddle from about 8 miles, with some erosion and seepage causing muddy patches and ruts in wet years. At about 8.8 miles the trail begins a gentle descent, with further logging and fire damage after 9 miles.

From about 9.6 miles the trail is marked by numerous large constructed drainages on either side, some of which may be confused with the actual trail, so pay close attention as you descend. GPS is highly recommended here. At 9.75 miles a large eroded gully marks the beginning of a stretch of trail in very bad condition. At 9.9 miles many timber roads join the trail and can cause confusion given the lack of signage; continue north and then curve west. The same occurs at 10.2 miles, the junction of which is marked by a brown post labeled "Beginners." Here the trail veers right (east), becoming very gravelly and very eroded shortly thereafter. At 10.4 miles there is another confusing, unmarked junction; here the trail goes straight (south) and not downhill, contrary to intuition.

After that junction the trail becomes easier to navigate, becoming mostly flat as it contours around the southeast face of the mountain to about 11 miles. There is considerably more deadfall in this section, but nothing impassable. At about 11.7 miles two wet drainages cross the trail but are easily forded, and the trail trends downhill.

At about 12.4 miles the trail takes a sharp left (southeast) downhill; an old timber road to the right (west) is "closed" by two metal fence posts. From here the trail becomes rough, rocky, and somewhat indistinct until it joins VC0201, marked by a brown post, at about 12.5 miles (see Redondo & Solitario Loops, 65). Turn left (east) onto VC0201 and continue downhill, enjoying views of Valle Grande as you descend.

The trail is clear and obvious all the way to its junction with VC02 (the backcountry access road) at 13.7 miles. If using a two-car shuttle, this is where the trail ends. If not, turn left (north) onto VC02, which is open to vehicle traffic, and follow it 3.4 miles to return to the trailhead at the north end of Valle Jaramillo where you started, at 17.1 miles.

Valle Toledo Loop

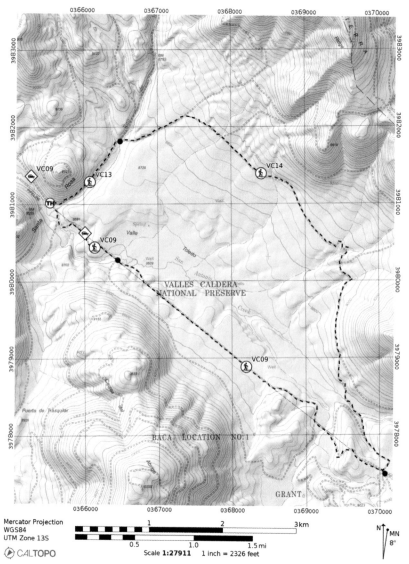

Mercator Projection
WGS84
UTM Zone 13S

⊙ CALTOPO

Scale **1:27911**   1 inch = 2326 feet

Valle Toledo Loop

A pleasant trail with minor elevation gain circling beautiful Valle Toledo, passing through young ponderosa groves and along San Antonio Creek.

Distance (RT): 9.5 miles
Elevation Range: 8,553–8,976 feet
Elevation Gain: 1,159 feet ascent
Difficulty: Easy to moderate
Recommended for Mountain Bikers: Yes
Conditions: The trail direction is best hiked clockwise as described below, especially for mountain bikers, but it should be done in reverse on foot in summer to avoid open meadows in the afternoon during monsoon season. While some may find the distance a bit long, the elevation gain is minor and the trail is otherwise not challenging. Signage is generally good and the trail is obvious, marked occasionally by brown posts. The burned area along VC14 does not quite reach the trail, so deadfall is very minor. However, the marked side trails along VC14 should not be entered due to hazardous burned areas. The burned trees at the junction of VC14 with VC09 have almost completely fallen, so very little threat of deadfall remains there. Do not attempt to cross Valle Toledo when thunderstorms are threatening. The last mile of VC09 is open to vehicle traffic. VC14 is alternating sun and shade; VC09 is full sun all day. Ground conditions are mostly gravelly, with occasional rocky patches. Sections of the trail contain large pieces of obsidian. Good

opportunities for elk sightings, bird-watching, and wildflowers. San Antonio Creek is a prime fishing spot. Collection of plants, antler sheds, obsidian, or other items is prohibited.

Trailhead: At the locked cable gate marked VC13, about 2.6 miles east of the T-junction of VC02–VC09 (the backcountry access roads).

Coordinates: 35° 57' 51.45" N, 106° 29' 28.17" W

UTM: 13S 365540 3981015

Hike Details

From the Entrance Station, take VC01–VC02 (the backcountry access roads) for approximately 12.6 miles to the T-junction; from there, turn right (east) onto VC09 (the backcountry access road) and continue driving for approximately 2.6 miles. Look for the locked cable gate marked VC13 on the left (north) side of the road. There is space to park at the trailhead (do not block the gate). The trail begins as a gravelly jeep road following Rito de los Indios Trail (97) northward, with a forested lava dome along the left (west) side of the trail. The exclosures along the stream to your right (east) are part of scientific studies of the riparian ecosystem. There are some seeps along the trail, after which at about 0.8 miles you will turn right (northeast) onto VC14, where you will need to hop across Rito de los Indios. The junction is marked with a brown post.

From the creek crossing, the trail begins a slight uphill climb, and at 1 mile it passes through an open iron gate. From here it levels out and passes through a grove of young ponderosa, and the trail is gravelly and in good condition. Occasionally, old timber roads veer off to the left (northeast), but the main trail is obvious. Just north of the trail is the edge of a large burned area, but it is not close enough to cause problems for hikers and bikers. At 1.8 miles VC1401 joins the trail from the left (northeast), marked with a brown post; while not officially closed, this trail (and trails VC1402 and VC1403 later on) pass through heavily burned areas and should not be entered due to the dangerous conditions.

The trees give way to views of Valle Toledo.

At about 2 miles the trees thin out and the trail crosses a pretty meadow, with views of Valle Toledo to the right (south) and the hills of the eastern rim of the caldera directly in front of you. In another 0.2 miles there is occasional deadfall, but it has been cleared from the trail. Until about 3 miles there are small burned areas on either side of the trail, alternating with healthy stands of trees.

At about 3.1 miles the trail takes a sharp bend right (south) and begins to curve around the hillside, with a few deep eroded gullies but nothing impassable. At 3.5 miles VC1402 joins the trail from the left (east); as noted above, do not follow this trail into the burned area but rather continue south on VC14. The trail then passes through another heavily burned area with the potential for deadfall, and at 3.6 miles it crosses a wide, eroded drainage. This is passable for hikers and bikers, but do not attempt to cross it when flowing or if rainstorms are in the area, as extremely dangerous flash floods can occur without warning.

Looking west across Valle Toledo.

At about 4 miles the trail enters a healthier stand of trees, and at 4.3 miles VC1403 joins the trail from the left (east). Again, do not follow this trail but rather continue south on VC14 as it trends downhill. At about 4.6 miles the trail passes through another open iron gate, drops down to a drainage, and offers a lovely view westward down Valle Toledo. After crossing the drainage, the trail turns left (east) and begins to ascend up a narrow valley along the backside of Cerro del Medio.

For the next three-quarters of a mile, the trail passes through burned areas as it ascends, with a few downed but passable trees and extensive ruts and gullies as it approaches the crest of the hill. At 5.4 miles the trail curves right (south), continuing through burned and eroded areas, until it reaches the junction with VC09 in another tenth of a mile. The marker for VC09 is somewhat to the left (east) of the actual junction and not immediately visible; the junction is at the crest of the hill, with the heavily burned north side of Cerro del Medio visible directly in front of you. Mountain bikers who wish to exit the preserve via the eastern rim of the caldera should continue east on VC09 to reach Cañada Bonita and Pajarito Mountain Ski Area (see Routes for Mountain Bikers, 168).

To continue our loop, turn right (northwest) at VC09. Here the trail is a clear jeep road (used by New Mexico Gas Company for a pipeline that serves the town of Los Alamos) and is very exposed; nearly all of the burned trees have fallen. Do not linger here if thunderstorms are threatening. A short ascent at about 5.8 miles brings you to the crest of a hill, after which the trail begins to descend rather steeply on loose rock and gravel before gradually leveling out at about 6 miles.

At about 6.3 miles the trail passes through another open iron gate and enters Valle Toledo. From here the trail rolls gently northwest across the valley, with the northeast side of Cerros del Abrigo on your left (south) and San Antonio Creek meandering on your right (north). From here to the end of the trail, a distance of about 3 more miles, the route is completely exposed and should not be attempted when thunderstorms are threatening.

At about 8.5 miles the trail passes a locked cable gate and reaches the parking area at the eastern end of VC09 (the backcountry access road). Continue on the road, which is open to vehicle traffic, to return to the trailhead at 9.5 miles.

Crossing Valle Toledo in early winter.

Rito de los Indios Trail

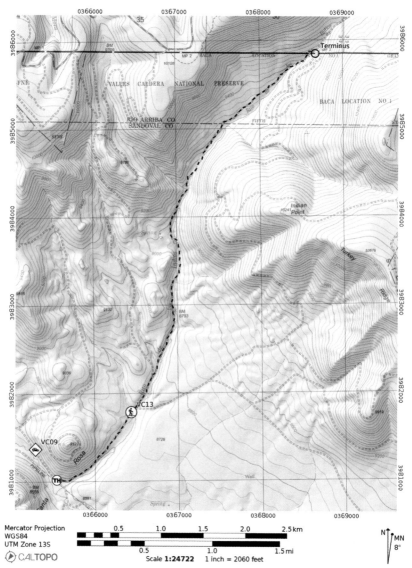

Mercator Projection
WGS84
UTM Zone 13S

CALTOPO

Scale **1:24722**   1 inch = 2060 feet

N MN
8°

Rito de los Indios Trail

A gentle out-and-back hike along an old jeep road following burbling Rito de los Indios, passing through dense groves of ponderosa pine and Douglas fir, and finishing just past a pretty, narrow valley at the preserve's northern boundary fence line.

Distance (RT): 7.8 miles
Elevation Range: 8,568–9,494 feet
Elevation Gain: 1,182 feet ascent
Difficulty: Easy to moderate
Recommended for Mountain Bikers: Yes, although the first half is entirely uphill.
Conditions: The trail is hiked or biked as an out-and-back, with a gentle ascent in the first half. Mountain bikers may find the long ascent challenging, but the downhill return is a great reward. Several streams cross the trail and lack planks or bridges but are easily forded. The trail is generally in good condition, and though lacking in signage the route is clear. Where present, signage is brown posts. The forest is dense and unhealthy, but burned areas are few and there is very little deadfall. The meadow should not be entered when thunderstorms are threatening. Alternating sun and shade. Ground conditions are generally gravelly, with some rocky patches. An old cabin, a ruined sawmill, and several dendro-glyphs (aspen carvings) may be seen along the way. Good opportunities for wildflowers, especially in the spring, and elk sightings and golden aspen in the autumn.

Trailhead: At the locked cable gate marked VC13, about 2.6 miles east of the T-junction of VC02–VC09 (the backcountry access roads).

Coordinates: 35° 57' 51.45" N, 106° 29' 28.17" W

UTM: 13S 365540 3981015

Hike Details

From the Entrance Station, take VC01–VC02 (the backcountry access roads) for approximately 12.6 miles to the T-junction; from there, turn right (east) onto VC09 (the backcountry access road) and continue driving for approximately 2.6 miles. Look for the locked cable gate marked VC13 on the left (north) side of the road. There is space to park at the trailhead (do not block the gate). The trail was reputedly used by the Bond family in the mid-twentieth century to access their ranching operations in the caldera, connecting to Forest Road 144 and then to Española, where they were based. The trail begins as a gravelly jeep road following Rito de los Indios northward, with a forested lava dome along the left (west) side of the trail. The exclosures along the stream to your right (east) are part of scientific studies of the riparian ecosystem. There are some seeps along the trail, and at about 0.8 miles, where VC14 (see Valle Toledo Loop, 91) branches off to the right (northeast), you will need to hop across a small stream. Shortly thereafter, the trail passes through an open metal gate and the road quality begins to deteriorate somewhat but is still clear. Ignore the old timber road branching off to your left (northwest) as you continue northward.

After about 1 mile the trail skirts a burned area on the left (west) of the trail and enters the first of several stands of Douglas fir. Just shy of 2 miles you will need to hop across another small stream as the trail passes a second, more heavily burned area on the right (east), although here the trail is not threatened by potential deadfall. From the stream for the next 0.2 miles the trail becomes very rocky and may be challenging for bikers. The trail then crosses a third stream and begins a steady uphill climb, but the grade is very

Bond cabin just off the main trail.

reasonable, and soon healthier forest returns, offering welcome shade. At about 2.5 miles yet another stream crosses the trail, after which a short side trail on the left (east) leads to an old cabin, built as a summer retreat away from the center of ranch operations in Valle Grande during the later Bond era. The cabin is unsafe to enter but is worth a look around.

Beyond the cabin the main trail is clear, with some patches of loose rocks, and as the tree density increases some dendroglyphs may be spotted on the aspen. These were carved by the shepherds and cowboys who tended the flocks and herds on the ranch during the twentieth century. Please do not be tempted to add your own!

At about 3 miles another small stream crosses the trail, and then the trees begin to give way as a narrow valley starts to open out.

Golden aspens in late autumn.

North valley of Rito de los Indios.

Here you will find the ruins of an old sawmill, a livestock corral, and the shell of a logging truck, along with various other detritus. While the clutter is unfortunate, it does not detract much from the beauty of the valley. As you continue up the valley, keep an eye out for more dendroglyphs on the aspen in the stands to your left (west). The elk particularly like these groves in the autumn.

At about 3.8 miles the trail reenters the forest and climbs steeply but briefly uphill, reaching the fence line in another tenth of a mile. This marks the northern boundary of the preserve and the end of the trail. Retrace the trail the way you came to return to the trailhead at 7.8 miles.

La Garita Summit Trail

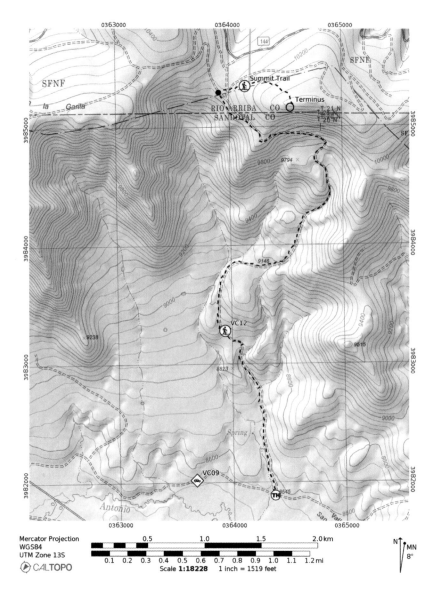

La Garita Summit Trail

A popular out-and-back trail that climbs up an old jeep road through forested groves and high-elevation meadows to the northern rim of the caldera, finishing at an open meadow and rewarding your efforts with stunning, sweeping views of the preserve.

Distance (RT): 7.6 miles
Elevation Range: 8,556–10,335 feet
Elevation Gain: 1,902 feet ascent
Difficulty: Strenuous
Recommended for Mountain Bikers: Yes, but very aerobically challenging due to the sustained and often steep 3.8-mile ascent, with extensive deadfall near the summit.
Conditions: The trail is hiked or biked as an out-and-back, with a sustained ascent for most of the first half. The trail fades out upon reaching the meadow at the overlook. Mountain bikers may wish to cross the meadow and reach the overlook on foot. While the trail is mostly easily navigated, trust-era yellow wooden mileage signposts are posted for ascending and descending directions, which can be very confusing. Signage from the fence line to the overlook is limited to arrows on the ground constructed from tree limbs, and they are easily missed. There is very little deadfall until the trail reaches the fence line; thereafter, some threatening standing dead trees could be dangerous in high winds. The trail should not be attempted if

thunderstorms are threatening. Full sun for much of the trail, especially in the higher regions. Ground conditions are mostly gravelly or rocky until reaching the grassy overlook. The overlook offers one of the finest viewpoints in the preserve. Good opportunities for wildlife and wildflowers.

Trailhead: At the locked cable gate marked VC12, about 1.6 miles east of the T-junction of VC02–VC09 (the backcountry access roads).

Coordinates: 35° 58' 20.29" N, 106° 30' 15.79" W

UTM: 13S 364361 3981922

Hike Details

From the Entrance Station, take VC01–VC02 (the backcountry access roads) for approximately 12.6 miles to the T-junction; from there, turn right (east) onto VC09 (the backcountry access road) and continue driving for approximately 1.6 miles. Look for the locked cable gate marked VC12 on the left (north) side of the road. There is space to park at the trailhead (do not block the gate). From here, the trail begins as a gravelly jeep road following a marshy stream. After half a mile, the trail crosses an eroded gully and soon trends left (north) as it begins to climb. Erosion along the edge of the trail continues for some distance, but the trail is wide enough to be easily passable. At three-quarters of a mile, hop across a small stream and continue uphill through pretty stands of ponderosa.

After about 1.5 miles the trail enters a small meadow and levels out briefly, with some seepage and deep ruts along the route. Approaching 2 miles, the trail skirts a burned area with some threatening standing dead trees, and it becomes rougher and rockier as the north ridgeline comes into view. At 2.3 miles the trees give way to a wide, open meadow, with the summit clearly visible in front of you. This is a great spot to take a break and catch your breath.

Windswept trees on the face of La Garita. Photo by Peter Dickson.

Leaving the meadow, the trail begins a sustained climb toward the ridgeline, switchbacking its way up and offering views south across the caldera, with even the Sandia Mountains in Albuquerque visible on a clear day. Just shy of 3 miles the trail passes through an open iron gate and enters another burned area, returning to pretty aspen groves as it curves north toward the fence line and gradually levels out.

At 3.25 miles a disused timber road veers off to the right (northeast); stay on the main trail for another tenth of a mile to reach the fence line and locked iron gate at the preserve boundary. Turn right (east) here and continue along the fence line, passing through burned areas with threatening standing dead trees. Caution should

View of Redondo Peak from La Garita summit.

be exercised when passing through here in high winds. At 3.6 miles a yellow wooden post indicates that the trail turns right (southeast) away from the fence line. Look for a large arrow on the ground constructed out of tree limbs. From here there is considerable deadfall blocking the trail. Mountain bikers may wish to dismount and continue on foot to the overlook. A second large ground arrow may be seen at 3.75 miles as the trail continues south toward the overlook.

At approximately 3.8 miles the trail becomes indistinct and fades out as the trees give way to a high meadow at the summit, with views encompassing nearly the entire caldera. This is the finest viewpoint in the preserve. Do not attempt the summit or linger in the open meadow if thunderstorms are threatening. Retrace the trail the way you came to return to the trailhead after 7.6 miles.

Northwest Rim Trail

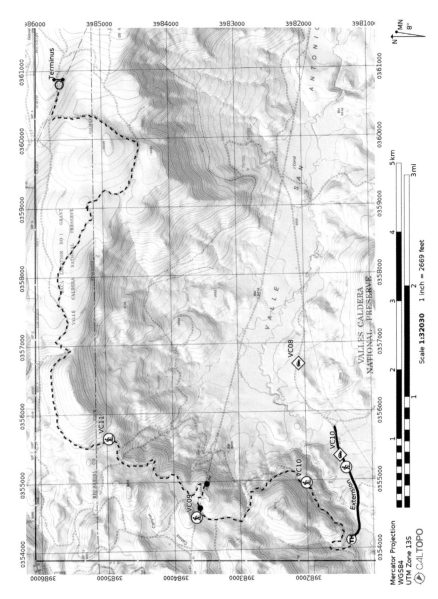

Northwest Rim Trail

The longest of the preserve's trails but a most rewarding one, with large groves of aspen, excellent opportunities for elk sightings, hidden high meadows, and a rarely seen view of Redondo Mountain.

Distance (RT): 18.6 miles (main trail); 21.2 miles (with Extension)

Elevation Range: 8,392–10,189 feet (main trail); 8,343–10,189 feet (with Extension)

Elevation Gain: 2,501 feet ascent (main trail); 2,741 feet ascent (with Extension)

Difficulty: Strenuous

Recommended for Mountain Bikers: Yes, with only minimal deadfall, but the entire first half is uphill, steeply at times.

Conditions: The trail is hiked or biked as an out-and-back, with sections of short ascents alternating with largely flat sections. Mountain bikers may find a few ascents challenging, but the downhill return is a great reward. There are a few sections with deep eroded gullies, though these are easily avoided, and with only minor deadfall this trail is ideal for trail runners. The trail is generally in good condition and is largely easy to follow despite poor signage, although a couple of junctions require close attention. Where present, signage is brown posts. The forest is dense and unhealthy and a fire is waiting to happen, but there are few burned areas and there is very little deadfall. This trail should not be attempted when the fire danger is high, and the meadows should be avoided when thunderstorms are threatening. The

Extension may be open to vehicle traffic. Alternating sun and shade, except in the meadows. Ground conditions vary, from sandy to grassy to loose rock. Good opportunities for elk sightings and golden aspen in the autumn.

Trailhead: At the locked cable gate marked VC10 after crossing San Antonio Creek, about 1.3 miles west of the junction of VC08–VC10 (the backcountry access roads). If the cable gate at the VC08–VC10 junction is unlocked, only high-clearance, four-wheel-drive vehicles should drive to the trailhead, as the road is in extremely poor condition and vehicle damage is likely.

Coordinates: 35° 57' 56.34" N, 106° 37' 7.53" W

UTM: 13S 354036 3981350

If the cable gate at the VC08–VC10 junction is locked or you do not have four-wheel drive, park your vehicle here (do not block the gate) and walk or ride 1.3 miles down the jeep road to reach the trailhead.

Extension Coordinates: 35° 58' 8.6" N, 106° 35' 54.12" W

Extension UTM: 13S 355881 3981697

Hike Details

From the Entrance Station, take VC01–VC02 (the backcountry access roads) for approximately 12.6 miles to the T-junction; from there, turn left (west) onto VC09 (the backcountry access road) and continue driving for approximately 4.2 miles. The backcountry access road becomes VC08 1.8 miles after the T-junction, and it reaches a junction with VC10 after another 2.4 miles. The cable gate here may or may not be unlocked (see Trailhead and Extension above). From the VC10 cable gate, the road heads largely downhill and is very eroded in places. After about a mile the road crosses San Antonio Creek, and it is lined on both sides by exclosures that are part of scientific studies of the riparian ecosystem. After about one-third of a mile more, find the trailhead on your right (north), marked by a brown post labeled VC10 and a locked cable gate. Park at the locked

View of Valle San Antonio through the trees.

cable gate (do not block the gate). The mileage as described below starts from this trailhead.

The trail proceeds up a narrow meadow toward groves of mixed ponderosa and aspen, and in about a tenth of a mile it turns sharply right (east). An old timber road continues straight (north); while this junction is unmarked, the correct trail is obvious. The trail heads gently uphill, becoming rocky in places, and contours around the hillside while trending northeast. In about half a mile, Valle San Antonio may be seen through the trees to the right (east).

The trail continues to contour, becoming sandier and quite eroded in places, with gullies beginning to wash out the edges. At about 1 mile a steep hillside to the left (west) is strewn with boulders and has the potential for rockfall. As the trail heads more steadily uphill, the gullies worsen and may be problematic for bikers. At about 1.2 miles the trail approaches the crest of the hill and a small meadow,

Trail junction at a small meadow.

and shortly thereafter it reaches a Y-junction. This is not marked but the trail turns obviously left (northwest), with a very faint right-hand trail proceeding straight (north). For the next tenth of a mile the trail is rockier with more eroded gullies, improving considerably as it levels out and begins to trend northward, offering another nice view of Valle San Antonio to the right (east).

At about 1.5 miles the trail resumes a gentle climb, entering a denser forest of Douglas fir. The climb becomes steeper and the trail becomes rockier and more eroded for the next tenth of a mile, eventually leveling out and reaching a pretty aspen grove at around 2 miles. For the next 0.2 miles the trail alternates between sand and rocks, with deep gullies as it heads uphill before crossing an open fence line, passing the ruins of a cabin on the right (east), and entering a small meadow with a few piles of roughhewn planks from a long-abandoned sawmill.

The trail curves right (north) as it crosses the meadow and reenters the trees, heading gently but steadily uphill for another 0.2 miles before reaching the junction with VC09 after about 2.4 miles. This is a very obvious jeep road marked by yellow New Mexico Gas Company warning posts (a gas pipeline runs beneath VC09 across the caldera, serving the town of Los Alamos) and a brown post labeled VC09 just to the right (east) of the junction.

Turn right (east) onto VC09 and head first uphill and then downhill to reach VC11 after about 0.4 miles. The trail is a slightly rutted track with minor deadfall. Turn left (north) onto VC11 and follow the trail as it levels out and passes through several lovely groves of aspen, very gradually contouring uphill. From about 3.25 miles Valle San Antonio may be spotted through the trees as the trail trends northward, occasionally curving left and right as it contours. At about 3.6 miles the trail curves sharply left (northwest), with glimpses of the ridgeline to the right (northeast). At 3.8 miles the trail begins a steady trend right (north), and from here occasional open patches among the trees offer good opportunities for elk sightings.

Just shy of 4 miles the trail reaches an unmarked Y-junction at the

Aspen grove in early morning autumn light.

edge of a meadow, but the correct direction is obvious on the ground as the trail heads right (northeast) and slowly up a rockier track. Shortly thereafter the trail levels out and curves right (east) before climbing again and curving left (north). At about 4.1 miles, some maps have an old timber road marked as branching right (south) from the trail, but this is no longer visible on the ground and should not cause problems. In another tenth of a mile the trail becomes less rocky and begins a slow climb, leveling out as it crosses into Rio Arriba County at about 4.4 miles.

From here the trail passes through a very dense and unhealthy area of forest, which should not be entered if the fire danger is high. At about 4.5 miles the trail begins to trend right (northeast), and at 4.8 miles the trail curves more sharply right, trending almost due east and slowly gaining elevation for some distance. The trail is easy to follow and is a clear dirt track with occasional loose rocks for the next half mile, until at about 5.4 miles when the trail begins to climb around a small drainage and becomes rockier. As it climbs around the drainage, the trail appears as a sharp V on maps, and at 5.6 miles it reaches the apex of the V and takes a sharp left (northeast) to climb steadily uphill. An old timber road going down the drainage is marked on some maps, but the main trail is obvious.

At 5.75 miles the trail curves sharply right (southeast) and becomes steeper over the next tenth of a mile, after which the trail levels out and the forest opens up as aspen groves begin to line the trail once more. Just shy of 6 miles, a half-buried cattle guard and several old fence posts may be seen to the right (south) of the trail, after which the trail reaches another unmarked Y-junction adjacent to a small pile of boulders. Go left (northeast) and uphill; take care, as the trail is full of loose rocks and some eroded gullies. In about 0.2 miles the trail reaches yet another unmarked Y-junction, but this time it goes right (east) and soon levels out. Shortly thereafter the trail resumes its gentle, steady climb, detouring around one large downed tree and then opening out a bit around 6.5 miles. From here the trail will be mostly full sun, especially in summer, despite the dense forest lining both sides of the trail.

Tree-lined trail.

For the next 0.5 miles the adjacent forest is dotted with small glades offering good opportunities for elk sightings. At about 7 miles the trail curves left (northeast), and at about 7.2 miles, after passing a large pile of waste timber, the trail enters a small clearing, curving right (south) as it crosses it. From here to the terminus the trail is very exposed and hikers and bikers should not continue if thunderstorms are threatening. After crossing the clearing the trail reenters Sandoval County and curves slightly left (southeast) as it heads gently downhill, passing a small burn and some scattered glades. At 7.4 miles the trail curves right (southwest) and soon enters a long narrow meadow, passing a cabin affectionately known as "the Hilton." This was used during the trust era by outfitters during hunting season and by wildlife officers conducting elk counts.

The trail continues southeast along the somewhat swampy meadow, curving slightly left (northeast) and uphill as it leaves the

Looking south from Northwest Rim Trail terminus.

meadow and enters part of the 2018 San Antonio burn at 7.9 miles. Do not linger here in high winds, as the standing dead trees pose a serious hazard. At about 8.1 miles the trail reaches an unmarked Y-junction at the edge of the burn; go left (north) and shortly thereafter skirt a meadow on the right (east), enjoying views of the ridgeline along the way. Over the next half mile the trail passes another pretty glade and crosses a second narrow meadow before it reenters Rio Arriba County at about 8.6 miles. The trail continues straight (north), passing an old timber road on the left (west) at 8.75 miles, before leaving the meadow and beginning to climb slowly uphill.

At about 8.9 miles an old timber road on the right (east) is marked on some maps but is not obvious on the ground. The correct trail clearly continues straight (north) and more steeply uphill, becoming rockier with some erosion and entering a dense forest. At 9 miles the trail curves sharply right (east) as it continues uphill, and it almost immediately reaches an unmarked T-junction. At the junction the trail continues right (east), with the northern boundary fence line just visible through the trees to the left (north). At

9.2 miles the trail enters a small meadow as both Redondo Mountain and the northern boundary gate come into view, reaching the terminus at the locked metal gate in another tenth of a mile.

Return the way you came, reaching VC09 at about 15.8 miles. Turn right (west) onto VC09 to reach VC10 at 16.2 miles, and then turn left (south) onto VC10 to return to the trailhead at about 18.6 miles. If hiking or biking the Extension, which may be open to vehicle traffic, turn left (east) onto the jeep road to return to your vehicle at 21.2 miles.

Northwest Corner Trail

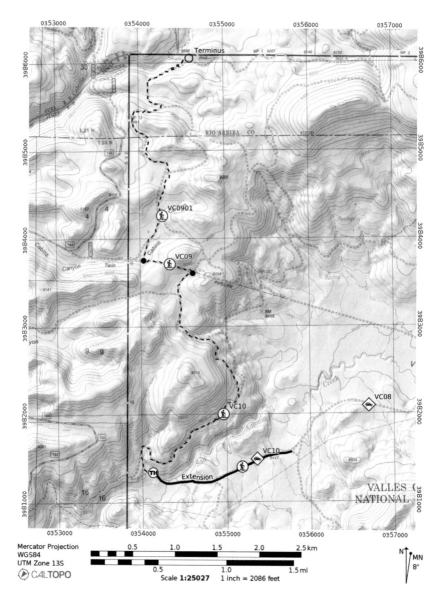

Mercator Projection
WGS84
UTM Zone 13S
CALTOPO

Scale **1:25027**   1 inch = 2086 feet

Northwest Corner Trail

A moderately challenging out-and-back hike in one of the least-visited areas of the preserve, through shady forests and charming hidden meadows, gently climbing from Valle San Antonio to reach the northwestern boundary of the preserve.

Distance (RT): 9.7 miles (main trail); 12.3 miles (with Extension)
Elevation Range: 8,392–9,020 feet (main trail); 8,343–9,020 feet (with Extension)
Elevation Gain: 1,484 feet ascent (main trail); 1,724 feet ascent (with Extension)
Difficulty: Moderate to strenuous
Recommended for Mountain Bikers: Yes, with only minimal deadfall, but the first half is almost entirely uphill, steeply at times.
Conditions: The trail is hiked or biked as an out-and-back, with sections of short ascents alternating with largely flat sections. Mountain bikers may find a few ascents challenging, but the downhill return is a great reward. There are a few sections with deep eroded gullies or downed trees, but these are easily navigated. The trail is generally in good condition and is largely easy to follow despite poor signage, although a couple of junctions require close attention. GPS is recommended. Where present, signage is brown posts. The forest is dense and unhealthy and a fire is waiting to happen, but there are no burned areas and there is very little deadfall. This trail should not be attempted when the

fire danger is high, and the meadows should be avoided when thunderstorms are threatening. The Extension may be open to vehicle traffic. Mostly shady, except in the meadows. Ground conditions vary, from sandy to grassy to rocky. Some dendroglyphs (aspen carvings) may be spotted from Twin Cabins Canyon to the boundary fence line, although they are easier to see on the return. Good opportunities for golden aspen in the autumn.

Trailhead: At the locked cable gate marked VC10 after crossing San Antonio Creek, about 1.3 miles west of the junction of VC08–VC10 (the backcountry access roads). If the cable gate at the VC08–VC10 junction is unlocked, only high-clearance, four-wheel-drive vehicles should drive to the trailhead, as the road is in extremely poor condition and vehicle damage is likely.

Coordinates: 35° 57' 56.34" N, 106° 37' 7.53" W
UTM: 13S 354036 3981350

If the cable gate at the VC08–VC10 junction is locked or you do not have four-wheel drive, park your vehicle here (do not block the gate) and walk or ride 1.3 miles down the jeep road to reach the trailhead.

Extension Coordinates: 35° 58' 8.6" N, 106° 35' 54.12" W
Extension UTM: 13S 355881 3981697

Hike Details

From the Entrance Station, take VC01–VC02 (the backcountry access roads) for approximately 12.6 miles to the T-junction; from there, turn left (west) onto VC09 (the backcountry access road) and continue driving for approximately 4.2 miles. The backcountry access road becomes VC08 1.8 miles after the T-junction, and it reaches a junction with VC10 after another 2.4 miles. The cable gate here may or may not be unlocked (see Trailhead and Extension above). From the VC10 cable gate, the road heads largely downhill and is very eroded in places. After about 1 mile the road crosses San Antonio

View of Redondito Peak from Valle San Antonio.

Creek and is lined on both sides by exclosures that are part of scientific studies of the riparian ecosystem. After about one-third of a mile more, find the trailhead on your right (north), marked by a brown post labeled VC10 and a locked cable gate. Park at the locked cable gate (do not block the gate). The mileage as described below starts from this trailhead.

The trail proceeds up a narrow meadow toward groves of ponderosa and aspen, and in about a tenth of a mile it turns sharply right (east). An old timber road continues straight (north); while this junction is unmarked, the correct trail is obvious. The trail heads gently uphill, becoming rocky in places, and contours around the hillside while trending northeast. In about half a mile, Valle San Antonio may be seen through the trees to the right (east).

The trail continues to contour, becoming sandier and quite eroded in places, with gullies beginning to wash out the edges.

Crossing an old fence line.

At about 1 mile a steep hillside to the left (west) is strewn with boulders and has the potential for rockfall. As the trail heads more steadily uphill the gullies worsen and may be problematic for bikers. At about 1.2 miles the trail approaches the crest of the hill and a small meadow, and shortly thereafter it reaches a Y-junction. This is not marked but the trail turns obviously left (northwest), with a very faint right-hand trail proceeding straight (north). For the next tenth of a mile the trail is rockier with more eroded gullies, improving considerably as it levels out and begins to trend northward, offering another nice view of Valle San Antonio to the right (east).

At about 1.5 miles the trail resumes a gentle climb, entering a denser forest of Douglas fir. The climb becomes steeper and the trail becomes rockier and more eroded for the next tenth of a mile, eventually leveling out and reaching a pretty aspen grove at around 2 miles. For the next 0.2 miles the trail alternates between sand and rocks, with deep gullies as it heads uphill before crossing an open fence line, passing the ruins of a cabin on the right (east), and entering a small meadow with a few piles of roughhewn planks from a long-abandoned sawmill.

The trail curves right (north) as it crosses the meadow and reenters the trees, heading gently but steadily uphill for another 0.2 miles before reaching the junction with VC09 after about 2.4 miles. This is a very obvious jeep road marked by yellow New Mexico Gas Company warning posts (a gas pipeline runs beneath VC09 across the caldera, serving the town of Los Alamos) and a brown post labeled VC09 just to the right (east) of the junction. Turn left (west) and continue along VC09 for about 0.3 miles to reach the junction with VC0901. This section is very badly eroded, particularly as the trail heads downhill; bikers should descend cautiously. The junction with VC0901 is marked by a brown post, but it is easy to miss as the post is a little obscured by trees. Turn right (north) onto VC0901 and head through a small grove of trees to reach Twin Cabins Canyon (which is really a meadow).

Twin Cabins Canyon.

The trail skirts the eastern edge of the meadow as it heads north, and at times it can be quite faint, especially in wet years when the undergrowth is thick. At about 3 miles the trail becomes easier to see, and shortly thereafter it passes the ruins of a cabin as it curves slightly right (east) and leaves the meadow. Just as the trail leaves the meadow, an unmarked old timber road joins the trail from behind and to the right (southeast); the main trail is very faint here but continues north and uphill. This junction is easily missed on the return; GPS will be helpful here.

As the trail leaves the meadow it becomes quite sandy and plagued by gullies as it climbs more steeply. At about 3.3 miles the trail reaches the crest of the hill and begins to head gently downhill. From here to the northwestern boundary fence, dendroglyphs may be seen on the aspen. These were carved by the shepherds and cowboys who tended the flocks and herds on the ranch during the twentieth century. Please do not be tempted to add your own! The trail soon levels out as it enters an extremely dense stretch of forest; this area should be avoided if the fire danger is high as it is a tinderbox. Over the next mile there are a few sections with deadfall, but these are very minimal and are easily navigated.

At about 3.5 miles small glades may be glimpsed through the trees, and the trail becomes very flat and sandy as it meanders northward. At about 3.8 miles the trail crosses into Rio Arriba County. At 4.2 miles the trail turns sharply left (north). An old timber road continues straight (east) at this unmarked junction, which may be confusing without GPS. Soon after the left turn, the trail trends downhill and gently curves right (north), entering a narrow meadow after about a tenth of a mile.

After crossing the meadow, the trail reenters the trees and becomes rockier with occasional deadfall. At about 4.5 miles the trail curves right (northeast), contouring gently around and down the hillside. The trail passes through an open iron gate, and after another 0.2 miles it enters a small meadow in the northwestern corner of the preserve. An abandoned car, a small stock pond, and the boundary fence are visible as the trail approaches the meadow. The trail then

Northwest Corner boundary fence line.

reaches an unmarked Y-junction with an old timber road; follow the trail left (north) a further tenth of a mile to reach the boundary fence and gate. Several large tree trunks on the edge of the meadow may serve as benches and make this a nice spot for a picnic.

Return the way you came, reaching VC09 at about 7 miles. Turn left (east) onto VC09 to reach VC10 at 7.3 miles, and then turn right (south) onto VC10 to return to the trailhead at about 9.7 miles. If hiking or biking the Extension, which may be open to vehicle traffic, turn left (east) onto the jeep road to return to your vehicle at 12.3 miles.

Cerro Seco Loop

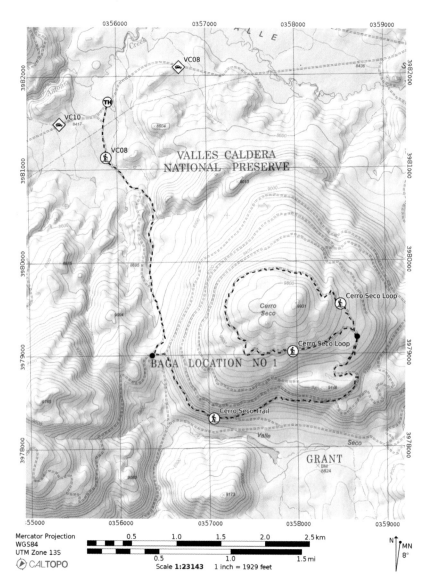

Mercator Projection
WGS84
UTM Zone 13S

CALTOPO

Scale **1:23143**   1 inch = 1929 feet

Cerro Seco Loop

A rewarding loop trail that contours around a lava dome after an initial long ascent up a pretty valley, offering views of Valle Seco and Valle San Antonio, as well as Redondo, Redondito, and Cerro Grande Peaks.

Distance (RT): 11.2 miles
Elevation Range: 8,394–9,706 feet
Elevation Gain: 1,664 feet ascent
Difficulty: Moderate to strenuous
Recommended for Mountain Bikers: Yes, with an initial aerobically challenging 2-mile ascent and a shorter, second ascent.
Conditions: The trail may be hiked or biked in either direction around Cerro Seco lava dome, but as hiked (counterclockwise) the best views are saved as a reward at the end of the loop. Mountain bikers will find the initial 2-mile ascent as well as the second ascent to the loop junction aerobically challenging, but the loop trail itself is easily bikeable and the return descent is great fun. While some may find the distance a bit long, the elevation gain is gradual and the loop trail is nearly flat. There is an old trust-era wooden trail marker at the junction of the loop trail with VC08, as well as yellow wooden signposts and two VC0803 brown posts, but several Y-junctions on the loop lack signage. A few places have the potential for rockfall. Threatening standing dead trees are minimal. The forest is extremely dense and a fire is waiting to happen, and it should not be entered if

the fire danger is high. This trail should not be attempted when thunderstorms are threatening. Alternating sun and shade. Ground conditions may be gravelly, rocky, or grassy. The south face of Cerro Seco offers impressive views. Good opportunities for wildflowers, and pikas if you're lucky, but fewer game trails are present here.

Trailhead: At the locked cable gate marked VC08, about 4.2 miles west of the T-junction of VC02–VC09 (the back-country access roads).

Coordinates: 35° 58′ 8.69″ N, 106° 35′ 53.54″ W

UTM: 13S 355895 3981700

Hike Details

From the Entrance Station, take VC01–VC02 (the backcountry access roads) for approximately 12.6 miles to the T-junction; from there, turn left (west) onto VC09 (the backcountry access road) and continue driving for approximately 4.2 miles. The backcountry access road becomes VC08 1.8 miles after the T-junction. Look for the locked cable gate marked VC08 on the left (south) side of the road. There is space to park at the trailhead (do not block the gate). From here, the trail is a somewhat sandy jeep road proceeding south across a rolling meadow, with Cerro Seco visible on the left (southeast) in front of you. After about three-quarters of a mile the trail begins to climb, entering groves of dense fir and aspen and paralleling a dry streambed on the right (west) of the trail. There are occasionally deep ruts in the trail, and mountain bikers may find some sections of this stretch difficult after recent precipitation. At about 1.4 miles the trees open out and the trail passes several meadows on either side of the route.

Just shy of 2 miles the trail reaches the junction with Cerro Seco Loop on the left (east) and San Antonio Mountain Trail (133) on the right (west). Both still have trust-era wooden trail markers. Mountain bikers who wish to connect with VC06 or continue on VC08 to connect with Sulfur Canyon should continue straight (south) here

Heading up the trail to Cerro Seco.

(see Routes for Mountain Bikers, 168). To continue our trail, take Cerro Seco Loop, ignoring the old timber road that veers to your left (northeast) shortly after the trail junction. Follow the sandy jeep road and contour eastward, watching out for occasional rockfall from the hillside. At about 2.5 miles the trees open out and offer nice views of Valle Seco below you and Redondito Peak opposite you to the right (south). The trail then reaches a Y-junction marked with a yellow wooden signpost, with an old timber road heading downhill to the right (southeast) and our trail heading uphill to the left (northeast).

At about 3 miles the views of Valle Seco return on your right (south), and the trail passes through a short stretch with potential for rockfall. At 3.4 miles the trail reaches another unmarked Y-junction and again heads uphill to the left (northeast); shortly thereafter the trail is joined by two timber roads and heads straight ahead (slightly northeast). After about 3.75 miles the trail begins to climb steadily, curving somewhat tightly up the lava dome for about a quarter mile.

Some sections of the trail have potential for rockfall.

At 4 miles the trail levels out at a Y-junction marked with a yellow wooden signpost and heads right (northeast), reaching a small glade and the junction with the loop trail at 4.25 miles. The trail is marked VC0803 and may be hiked or biked in either direction; to go counterclockwise and save the best views for last, take the right-hand trail (north). The trail is very exposed here, so caution is advised when thunderstorms are threatening. There are occasionally some eroded gullies along the edge of the trail, but for the most part it is clear and wide for the entire loop around the lava dome. Within 0.3 miles the trail levels out and proceeds to contour gently around Cerro Seco.

At 4.6 miles the trail reaches another Y-junction marked with a yellow wooden signpost; take the right-hand trail heading west. If using US Forest Service or US Geological Survey maps, this junction can appear a little confusing. The trail enters a very dense stand of aspen, fir, and ponderosa, but at about 5 miles the trees begin to open out, yielding glimpses of Valle San Antonio and the northwestern rim of the caldera. This area should be avoided if the fire danger

Expansive views looking southeast along Cerro Seco Loop.

is high as it is a tinderbox. After this there is another short stretch with potential for rockfall, as well as the occasional juniper bush growing in the middle of the trail.

At about 6 miles the trail crosses the first of three pretty drainages, with narrow glades hemmed in by fir and aspen. After another half mile, as the trail returns along the south face of Cerro Seco, the trees give way to expansive views of Redondo and Redondito Peaks, as well as the southeastern region of the caldera. This is the best viewpoint on the trail. The trail is very exposed here, so keep an eye on the weather.

At about 6.8 miles the trail enters a pretty meadow, after which the loop ends and rejoins the trail that brought you up from VC08. Turn right (south) and retrace the trail downhill to VC08. At 9.2 miles, rejoin VC08 and turn right (north), following it approximately 2 miles downhill to return to the trailhead at 11.2 miles.

San Antonio Mountain Trail

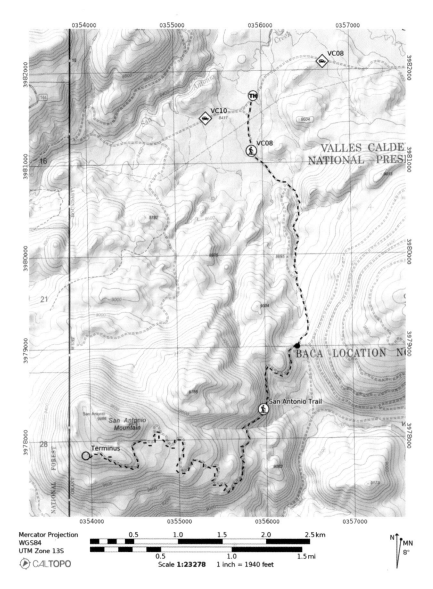

Mercator Projection
WGS84
UTM Zone 13S

CALTOPO

Scale **1:23278**   1 inch = 1940 feet

N MN 8°

San Antonio Mountain Trail

A pretty out-and-back hike through dense forest and small high-elevation meadows, offering good views of Valle Seco and Redondo and Redondito Peaks, ending just below the summit of San Antonio Mountain near the western boundary of the preserve.

Distance (RT): 11 miles
Elevation Range: 8,394–9,922 feet
Elevation Gain: 1,830 feet ascent
Difficulty: Moderate to strenuous
Recommended for Mountain Bikers: Yes, but the first half is entirely uphill, steeply at times.
Conditions: The trail is hiked or biked as an out-and-back, with a sustained ascent for most of the first half. The elevation gain is gradual but steady, and it will be aerobically challenging for bikers. The trail is in good condition and generally easy to follow, with a trust-era wooden trail marker at the junction of the trail with VC08, and yellow wooden posts marking both ascending and descending directions of travel. A couple of junctions near the summit are not well marked. Threatening standing dead trees are minimal. The forest is extremely dense and a fire is waiting to happen, and it should not be entered if the fire danger is high. This trail should not be attempted when thunderstorms are threatening. Alternating sun and shade. Ground conditions may be gravelly, rocky, or grassy, with some ruts and gullies but nothing impassable. The south face of San Antonio

Mountain offers impressive views. Interesting rock formations dot the trail, and an old fence-crew cabin may be seen just before the terminus. Good opportunities for wildflowers, but fewer game trails are present here.

Trailhead: At the locked cable gate marked VC08, about 4.2 miles west of the T-junction of VC02–VC09 (the backcountry access roads).

Coordinates: 35° 58' 8.69" N, 106° 35' 53.54" W

UTM: 13S 355895 3981700

Hike Details

From the Entrance Station, take VC01–VC02 (the backcountry access roads) for approximately 12.6 miles to the T-junction; from there, turn left (west) onto VC09 (the backcountry access road) and continue driving for approximately 4.2 miles. The backcountry access road becomes VC08 1.8 miles after the T-junction. Look for the locked cable gate marked VC08 on the left (south) side of the road. There is space to park at the trailhead (do not block the gate). From here, the trail is a somewhat sandy jeep road proceeding south across a rolling meadow, with San Antonio Mountain visible on the right (southwest) in front of you. After about three-quarters of a mile the trail begins to climb, entering groves of dense fir and aspen and paralleling a dry streambed on the right (west) of the trail. There are occasionally deep ruts in the trail, and mountain bikers may find some sections of this stretch difficult after recent precipitation. At about 1.4 miles the trees open out and the trail passes several meadows on either side of the route.

Just shy of 2 miles the trail reaches the junction with Cerro Seco Loop (127) on the left (east) and San Antonio Mountain Trail on the right (west). Both still have trust-era wooden trail markers. Mountain bikers who wish to connect with VC06 or continue on VC08 to connect with Sulfur Canyon should continue straight (south) here (see Routes for Mountain Bikers, 168). To continue our trail, take San Antonio Mountain Trail and follow it as it heads slightly southward and begins to curve gently uphill through dense stands of

View of Valle Seco through the trees.

Douglas fir and ponderosa. The trail is well defined and easy to follow, although occasionally there are eroded gullies and stretches of loose rocks and gravel. In wet years there is a profusion of wildflowers along much of the route.

At about 2.6 miles a few gaps in the trees offer nice views of Valle Seco to the left (east) of the trail. At 2.8 miles the trail curves sharply left (south), crossing a narrow drainage, and at about 3 miles the trail curves right (northwest) and begins to switchback more tightly up the mountain. At 3.2 miles Redondo and Redondito Peaks may be seen to the left (south). From here the trail becomes quite rutted and rocky, and it begins to climb more steeply for another 0.2 miles before briefly leveling out at an overlook with impressive views of Redondo Mountain and Jemez Valley.

From the overlook the trail resumes its climb, becoming sandy and rocky, with interesting rock formations scattered among the

Looking southwest toward Jemez Valley.

trees. At 3.6 miles the trail takes a sharp right (north) and begins to level out as it enters the first of several small, pretty meadows. More switchbacks ensue, and the trail becomes steeper again and more eroded after about 3.8 miles. From here the trail is increasingly exposed; hikers and bikers should exercise caution if thunderstorms are threatening.

After about 4 miles the trail levels out along a very pretty stretch as it passes through groves of trees and more small meadows. The trail resumes switchbacking but more gently now, leveling out again after another half mile. At 4.6 miles an old timber road joins the trail from the right (north), and a downtrail yellow wooden post makes this junction slightly confusing. Follow the main trail toward the left (south) and continue uphill. A similar situation occurs at 4.9 miles; again, follow the main trail toward the left (south) and continue uphill.

Narrow glade along San Antonio Mountain Trail.

From 5 miles the trail continues its switchbacks uphill, passing an old fence-crew cabin at about 5.3 miles and reaching the terminus at a small clearing bounded by trees and large boulders at about 5.5 miles. While this is not the actual summit of the mountain, it is very close; as before, hikers and bikers should exercise caution if thunderstorms are threatening.

Retrace your steps to return the way you came. At 9 miles, rejoin VC08 and turn left (north), following it approximately 2 miles downhill to return to the trailhead at about 11 miles.

Sulfur & Alamo Canyons Loop

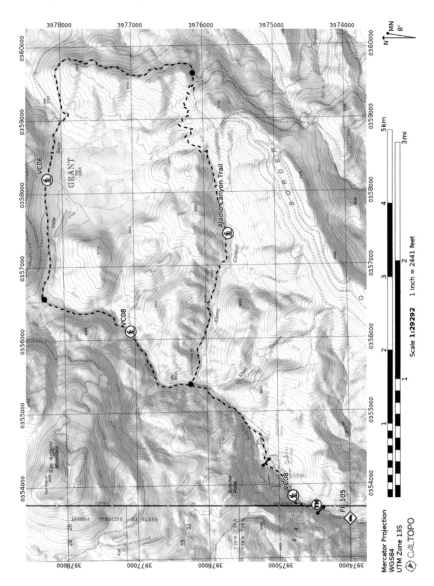

Sulfur & Alamo Canyons Loop

A delightful trail passing through varied terrain, from otherworldly sulfur fields to pretty creek-lined meadows to beautiful Valle Seco and Alamo Canyon, offering great views of several valleys and peaks.

Distance (RT): 12.2 miles
Elevation Range: 8,069–9,392 feet
Elevation Gain: 1,768 feet ascent
Difficulty: Moderate to strenuous
Recommended for Mountain Bikers: Yes, until Alamo Canyon, which is impassable to bikers due to extensive deadfall, although plans are in the works to clear this section. Once cleared, the full loop will be great.
Conditions: The trail is best hiked or biked clockwise as described below, passing through Valle Seco early in the day and returning via Alamo Canyon (currently impassible to bikers), especially in summer to avoid open meadows in the afternoon during monsoon season. While some may find the distance a bit long, the elevation gain is gradual. Most of the trail is obvious, although signage is minimal. Where present, signage is brown posts and occasional trust-era wooden trail markers and yellow posts. Signage along Alamo Canyon Trail is extremely poor. The primary difficulty is the first half mile of Alamo Canyon Trail, which is nearly impossible to discern; GPS is essential here. Hikers who get off track here may become disoriented quickly among the deadfall and numerous drainages. In wet years, parts of

lower Alamo Canyon may also be difficult to discern due to dense undergrowth, but as long as hikers follow the drainage downhill, it is not too challenging. Standing dead trees along sections of VC06 pose a threat in high winds. Hikers and bikers should not linger at Valle Seco, other meadows, or along ridgelines when thunderstorms are threatening. Alternating sun and shade. Ground conditions may be gravelly or grassy, and there are stretches of extensive deadfall in Alamo Canyon (although plans are in the works to clear this section). This region of the preserve has not suffered from much wildfire and is one of the prettiest areas in the backcountry. Many fumaroles and three geothermal ponds may be seen soon after the start of the hike and in Alamo Canyon. Good opportunities for prairie dogs as well as elk sightings at higher elevations, and profuse wildflowers at lower elevations.

Trailhead: At the locked iron gate marked VC08 about 2 miles from the junction of Sulfur Creek Road/Forest Road 105 and NM 4 (at mile marker 27).

Coordinates: 35° 54′ 13.04″ N, 106° 37′ 15.55″ W

UTM: 13S 353721 3974472

Hike Details

From NM 4, take Sulfur Creek Road (on the northeast side of the highway, at mile marker 27) and then turn immediately right onto Forest Road 105. Follow FR 105 for 2 miles to the VCNP locked iron gate. Park here (do not block the gate) and hop the fence. From the locked gate, the trail is marked as VC08 and is a jeep road, slightly eroded in places, climbing steadily along the creek. At 0.5 miles the trail enters a formerly private inholding and passes through an old sulfur mining area. This is also where the first exploratory geothermal wells in the preserve were drilled in the 1960s. Fumaroles and a sulfurous pond may be seen here, as well as various mining detritus, but hikers and bikers should be cautious when exploring sulfur fields

Hot spring flowing through sulfur-coated rocks.

and fumaroles. At 1 mile the trail reaches a second VCNP iron gate (which may or may not be locked), with trail quality improving once past the gate. Note the volcanic formations on the left (north) just across the creek, complete with caves.

The trail then begins to climb slightly as it crosses over the creek and passes through small meadows and pretty groves of ponderosa and Douglas fir. The exclosures along the creek to your right (southeast) are part of scientific studies of the riparian ecosystem. At the end of the third exclosure, at about 1.7 miles, the trail reaches the junction with Alamo Canyon Trail on your right (east). A trust-era wooden trail marker and a small turnaround with wooden beams on the ground blocking any vehicle traffic mark the junction. This is where you will rejoin VC08 on your return. Continue straight, heading north up the valley.

At about 2 miles the trail curves gently to the right (northeast), skirting marshy areas with grasses and wildflowers all along the creek. The trail proceeds to climb very gently after about half a mile,

Side valley along Sulfur Canyon.

with pretty valleys revealing themselves on either side of the route, as well as a small pond near the 3-mile mark.

At 3.3 miles the trail reaches the junction with VC06. Mountain bikers who wish to connect with the east–west backcountry access road should continue straight (north) here (see Routes for Mountain Bikers, 168). To continue our loop, take VC06 to the right (east), passing a locked cable gate and brown post. From here the sandy trail heads almost due east, entering a narrow valley lined with ponderosa and Douglas fir. Just shy of 4 miles a beautifully blue stock pond comes into view on the right (south), and then gorgeous Valle Seco opens out as the trail continues eastward for about a mile.

At 5 miles the trail reaches an unmarked Y-junction. VC06 continues to the right (southeast), uphill, and past a yellow flash flood warning sign. The trail enters a nicely shaded ponderosa grove as

Stock pond in beautiful Valle Seco.

it begins to climb, switchbacking gently up the hillside. In about a tenth of a mile the trail skirts a burned area, becoming rougher and steeper. The northern rim of the caldera may be seen through the trees to the left (north). At 5.5 miles the trail levels off a bit and curves sharply right (south), then resumes climbing gently. There are many game trails along this section, and elk sightings are likely.

After about 6.2 miles the forest opens out, offering views of Valle San Luis and the backside of Redondo Mountain to the left (southeast). There are a few sections of threatening standing dead trees along the trail, so caution is advised if hiking or biking through here in high winds. At 6.8 miles the trail curves sharply right (west) and offers a striking view of Redondito Peak, and after another 0.2 miles the trail reaches the junction with Alamo Canyon and Redondo

Border Trails (147). Mountain bikers who wish to connect with VC03 for Valle Jaramillo or Redondo Creek should continue straight (south) here (see Routes for Mountain Bikers, 168).

The junction of VC06 with Alamo Canyon and Redondo Border Trails is not entirely clear from VC06; while Redondo Border Trail still has a trust-era wooden trail marker, this is not immediately visible from VC06. The Alamo Canyon junction is defined by a small clearing to the right (northwest), marked by a low berm and an unmarked post, with VC06 continuing on to the left (south). Climb up and over the berm, and aim for the trees in front of you. Some arrows made of downed tree limbs have been placed on the ground to indicate direction, but there is no guarantee they will be there for long. Alamo Canyon Trail is currently impassable to bikers, although plans are in the works to clear this section.

The initial stretch of Alamo Canyon Trail is extremely difficult to follow. There is a great deal of overgrowth, particularly in wet years, as well as significant deadfall. GPS is critical here; beware of losing the trail for the first half mile down Alamo Canyon. Bear left (west) shortly after entering the trees, aiming to contour, and don't go down the drainage. (If you do go down the drainage, you will end up in the southeast corner of Valle Seco, which will make for a very long day.) After about 0.5 miles the trail becomes more recognizable as an old jeep road, but for nearly three-quarters of a mile it is plagued by deadfall as it contours slowly down the hillside. None of it is impassable to hikers, but it is tedious.

At about 8 miles the trail turns sharply left (south) as it passes a couple of old spools of barbed wire, proceeding quickly downhill and reaching the eastern edge of Alamo Canyon. For the next half mile or so, the trail is very indistinct and covered in dense grasses. Aim for the middle of the valley and simply head downhill due west, passing through a few small groves of trees and reaching the first of three ponds at about 8.6 miles. From here, despite deadfall the trail becomes easier to see as it parallels the creek downhill, crossing an eroded section dotted with a few small sulfurous fumaroles just shy of 9 miles. Shortly thereafter the trail passes a second, bubbling

Geothermal pond in Alamo Canyon.

sulfurous pond, and then it crosses an old wellhead flat adjacent to
an abandoned sulfur mine cut into the hillside.

At about 9.5 miles the trail becomes an obvious jeep road; on
many GPS systems, as well as US Forest Service and US Geological
Survey maps, this is marked as the eastern end of Alamo Canyon
Trail. Continue westward, crossing a pretty meadow home to a small
prairie dog colony. At about 9.8 miles the valley starts to open out
into a marshy meadow, and the third pond may be seen a short distance down the trail. The trail reaches the remarkably blue, bubbling
pond at about 10 miles, and about 0.3 miles later it crosses a stark,
wide sulfur flat.

At about 10.5 miles the trail reaches the exclosure adjacent to
the junction with VC08. Turn left (southwest) to return down Sulfur
Canyon and reach the trailhead at 12.2 miles.

Redondo Border Trail

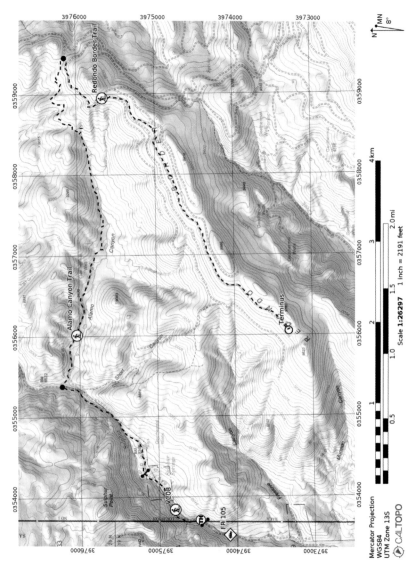

Redondo Border Trail

A long but otherwise moderately challenging out-and-back hike encompassing a wide variety of landscapes, from sulfurous fields with steaming fumaroles, to bubbling geothermal ponds, to sweeping views toward the northern rim of the caldera.

Distance (RT): 15.9 miles
Elevation Range: 8,069–9,732 feet
Elevation Gain: 2,028 feet ascent
Difficulty: Strenuous
Recommended for Mountain Bikers: Yes, once extensive deadfall is cleared, but the majority is currently impassable to bikers.
Conditions: The trail is hiked or biked as an out-and-back, and while the distance is long, the elevation gain is gradual. The trail is largely easy to follow, except for sections of Alamo Canyon Trail near the junction with VC06, where it is nearly impossible to discern (and particularly difficult on the return); GPS is essential here. Hikers who get off track here may become disoriented quickly among the deadfall and numerous drainages. In wet years, parts of lower Alamo Canyon may also be difficult to discern due to dense undergrowth, but as long as hikers follow the drainage up- and downhill, it is not too challenging. Signage along Alamo Canyon Trail is extremely poor. There are numerous trust-era yellow wooden signposts remaining along the Redondo Border section, although the ascending and descending mileage and directional signposts may cause some confusion. Do not linger in

open meadows or along ridgelines, particularly the Redondo Border section, when thunderstorms are threatening, or in areas of standing dead trees during high winds. Alternating sun and shade. Ground conditions may be gravelly or grassy, and there are stretches of extensive deadfall in Alamo Canyon (although plans are in the works to clear this section). Many fumaroles and three geothermal ponds may be seen soon after the start of the hike and in Alamo Canyon. Good opportunities for prairie dogs as well as elk at higher elevations, and profuse wildflowers at lower elevations.

Trailhead: At the locked iron gate marked VC08 about 2 miles from the junction of Sulfur Creek Road/Forest Road 105 and NM 4 (at mile marker 27).

Coordinates: 35° 54' 13.04" N, 106° 37' 15.55" W

UTM: 13S 353721 3974472

Hike Details

From NM 4, take Sulfur Creek Road (on the northeast side of the highway, at mile marker 27) and then immediately turn right onto Forest Road 105. Follow FR 105 for 2 miles to the VCNP locked iron gate. Park here (do not block the gate) and hop the fence. From the locked gate, the trail is marked as VC08 and is a jeep road, slightly eroded in places, climbing steadily along the creek. At 0.5 miles the trail enters a formerly private inholding and passes through an old sulfur mining area. This is also where the first exploratory geothermal wells in the preserve were drilled in the 1960s. Fumaroles and a sulfurous pond may be seen here, as well as various mining detritus, but hikers and bikers should be cautious when exploring sulfur fields and fumaroles. At 1 mile the trail reaches a second VCNP iron gate (which may or may not be locked), with trail quality improving once past the gate. Note the volcanic formations on the left (north) just across the creek, complete with caves.

The trail then begins to climb slightly as it crosses over the creek and passes through small meadows and pretty groves of ponderosa

A steaming fumarole along Sulfur Creek.

and Douglas fir. The exclosures along the creek to your right (southeast) are part of scientific studies of the riparian ecosystem. At the end of the third exclosure, at about 1.7 miles, the trail reaches the junction with the Alamo Canyon trailhead. A trust-era wooden trail marker and a small turnaround with wooden beams on the ground blocking any vehicle traffic mark the junction. Mountain bikers who wish to connect with the east–west backcountry access road should continue straight (north) here (see Routes for Mountain Bikers, 168). To continue on our trail, turn right (east) here to head up the canyon. In about a tenth of a mile the trail passes a wide sulfur flat on the right (south) and begins to trend slightly uphill.

Once past the sulfur flat, the trail opens out to a beautiful marshy meadow and is easy to follow. At 2.2 miles the trail passes a bubbling, remarkably blue geothermal pond. Apart from a few minor eroded gullies, this stretch of the trail is in good condition, although in wet years high grasses can obscure the path somewhat. At about 2.5 miles the trail passes an old geothermal wellhead and then becomes quite gravelly as it begins a steadier climb uphill. From here, erosion increases and the first of many downed trees block the trail. The trail then crosses a marshy meadow home to a prairie dog colony and continues

Heading east along a marshy meadow in the early morning.

to climb gently, reaching an old wellhead flat adjacent to an abandoned sulfur mine cut into the hillside at about 2.8 miles. On many GPS systems, as well as US Forest Service and US Geological Survey maps, this is marked as the eastern end of Alamo Canyon Trail. Cross the wellhead flat and continue east into the trees, passing another bubbling, sulfurous pond in about a tenth of a mile.

From the pond the trail climbs a bit more steeply and is plagued by deadfall, becoming a grassy track and somewhat faint after 3 miles. At 3.25 miles the trail is eroded by the creek and a few small sulfurous fumaroles. Beyond this, the trees open out into a narrow meadow with a third pond to your right (south). Thick undergrowth makes the trail difficult to discern here, and it becomes increasingly faint as it heads up the canyon. At 3.6 miles the trail passes through a small mixed grove of trees before entering the last meadow, with the grade becoming steeper now. The trail is very faint here, so aim for the trees and trend right (southeast). At 3.9 miles the trail switchbacks left (north) and is clearly an old jeep road; follow this as it climbs up the hillside and becomes rockier.

At about 4 miles the trail crests the hill, passes a couple of old spools of barbed wire, and takes a sharp right (southeast). From here

Beginning the climb out of Alamo Canyon.

the trail contours gently up and around the hill, and until reaching the junction with VC06 it is plagued by extensive deadfall as it passes through burned areas (although plans are in the works to clear this section). None of it is impassable to hikers, but it is tedious. Caution is advised when passing through here in high winds. At about 4.5 miles the jeep road is very indistinct and it is easy to get lost here; when in doubt, head uphill and aim for the skyline due east. GPS is strongly recommended. At 4.8 miles the trail is almost completely invisible, but the crest of the hill may be seen just ahead of you. As you exit the trees, the junction with VC06 is directly ahead and just down the small berm. Be sure to note where you exited the trees to join VC06, as the trail can be difficult to spot on your return. Mountain bikers who wish to reach Valle Seco should turn left (north) onto VC06 here, or turn right (south) to connect with VC03 for Valle Jaramillo or Redondo Creek (see Routes for Mountain Bikers, 168). To continue on our trail, take the junction with Redondo Border Trail, which is just to the right (southwest) and is the higher of two jeep roads. There is a trust-era Redondo Border wooden trailhead marker, but it is in very poor condition and may not last much longer.

Once on Redondo Border Trail, navigation becomes considerably

Looking southeast from the junction of Alamo Canyon, VC06, and Redondo Border Trails.

easier. There is some deadfall along the length of the trail, but it is not nearly as extensive as it is in upper Alamo Canyon. At about 5 miles Valle Seco may be seen to the right (north), and from there the trail enters a stand of healthy trees and contours mostly very gently uphill, trending southwestward. At about 5.3 miles the trail bends sharply left (southwest) at an overlook offering fine views in nearly every direction, and just past the overlook there is a pretty meadow below the trail.

At about 5.4 miles the trail reaches the first of many Y-junctions with old timber roads. Depending on which maps you are using, these disused roads may or may not be listed, and they can be confusing regardless. Fortunately, most of these junctions still have trust-era yellow wooden signposts indicating the correct direction, although they are generally found some yards after the actual junction, so pay careful attention as you go. Most of the time (but not always!), the correct trail is the one going uphill. At this first junction, take the right (southwest) trail, and about a tenth of a mile later, at the next Y-junction, take the left (southwest) trail.

At 5.75 miles take the left (southwest) trail at the Y-junction, and in another tenth of a mile take the right (west) trail at the next Y-junction. The trail now becomes a bit more gravelly and skirts a few burned areas, offering great views northward toward Valle Seco and the northern rim of the caldera. At about 6.3 miles deadfall increases and the trail becomes considerably overgrown as it passes through a grove of threatening standing dead trees. After another half mile the trail is clearer, passing through another burned area with nice views to the right (north).

At 7 miles the trail enters a dense grove of trees, and at 7.4 miles the trail is once more overgrown and plagued by deadfall. Despite this, the jeep road is still distinct, and it continues to a wooden terminus signpost just shy of 8 miles.

Retrace the trail the way you came, reaching the berm at the Alamo Canyon trailhead at 11.1 miles. Climb up and over the berm, and aim for the trees in front of you. Some arrows made of downed tree limbs have been placed on the ground to indicate direction, but there is no guarantee they will be there for long. GPS is critical here; beware of losing the trail for the first half mile down Alamo Canyon. Bear left (west) shortly after entering the trees, aiming to contour, and don't go down the drainage. (If you do go down the drainage, you will end up in the southeast corner of Valle Seco, which will make for a very long day.) Continue down Alamo Canyon Trail to rejoin VC08 at 14.2 miles, turning left (southwest) to return down Sulfur Canyon and reach the trailhead at 15.9 miles.

View of Valle Seco from Redondo Border Trail.

Redondo Creek–Mirror Pond Trail

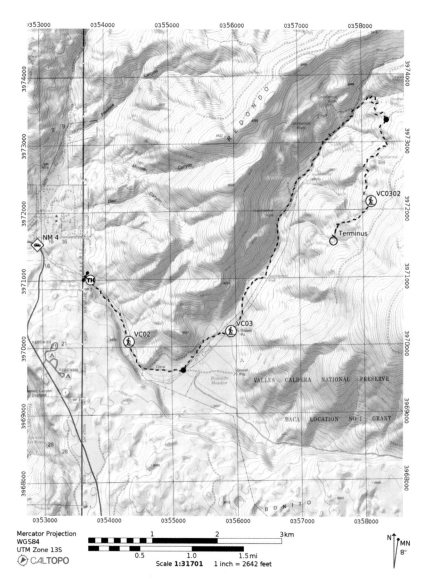

Redondo Creek–Mirror Pond Trail

An out-and-back hike following Redondo Creek, gently ascending up a valley until a short, steep climb gives way to a gentler trail that largely contours around Redondo Mountain before terminating at Mirror Pond.

Distance (RT): 13.9 miles
Elevation Range: 7,845–9,344 feet
Elevation Gain: 2,395 feet
Difficulty: Strenuous
Recommended for Mountain Bikers: Yes for VC02 and VC03, but miserably steep for about 1 mile prior to the junction with VC0302. Yes for VC0302 to Mirror Pond, once deadfall is cleared.
Conditions: The trail is hiked or biked as an out-and-back, and while the distance is long, the elevation gain is gradual except for a short, sustained climb prior to the junction with VC0302. Game sightings, including bears, are likely, particularly along VC0302, so hikers and bikers should be alert to their surroundings. Signage is minimal, but the trail is generally easy to follow. Where present, signage is brown posts. Narrow stretches of the trail along the creek may be dangerous in rainstorms, and the steep section and VC0302 should be avoided when thunderstorms are threatening due to elevation and exposure. Burned sections with standing dead trees pose a threat in high winds. Alternating sun and shade until the trail begins to climb steeply, after which it is largely

full sun. Ground conditions may be gravelly or rocky until reaching VC0302, which is currently unmaintained, more eroded, and plagued by deadfall. As the trail approaches Mirror Pond, ground conditions improve and may be gravelly or grassy. The old offices of Union Geothermal Company of New Mexico and numerous wellheads may be seen in the valley along Redondo Creek, but the structures should not be entered because they are in poor and dangerous condition. Good opportunities for wildflowers along the creek, and wildlife along VC0302. If you're lucky, you may catch a glimpse of the feral horse that makes Redondo Meadow its pasture.

Trailhead: At the locked iron gate at the VCNP Redondo Meadow Staging Area on the east side of NM 4 (at mile marker 28), at the jeep road marked VC02.

Coordinates: 35° 52' 22.36" N, 106° 37' 16.46" W

UTM: 13S 353641 3971063

Hike Details

From NM 4, turn off at the sign for the VCNP Redondo Meadow Staging Area (on the east side of the highway, near mile marker 28). Park at the locked iron gate (do not block the gate), and hop the fence, joining VC02 as it follows Redondo Creek up the valley. After about a mile the trail reaches the western edge of Redondo Meadow, and at about 1.5 miles the trail splits at a Y-junction. Mountain bikers who wish to connect with Banco Bonito Loop (161) should continue straight (east) here (see Routes for Mountain Bikers, 168). To continue on our trail, take the unmarked left fork northeast for VC03 and follow the jeep road as it climbs gently through pockets of ponderosa. At about 1.8 miles the trail passes through a burned stand of ponderosa, some of which are threatening the trail. Shortly thereafter, pick your way across a stream that crosses the trail.

After crossing the stream the trail enters a lovely grove of ponderosa, and at 2 miles an unmarked timber road veers off to the right

Heading up the valley along Redondo Creek.

(east). Continue on the main trail as it continues to climb, and as the trees open out you may catch a glimpse of impressive rimrocks on the ridge to your left (west). At about 2.7 miles the trail enters a narrow, pretty valley marked by old geothermal wells and Redondo Creek.

At 3 miles the trail passes by the abandoned offices of Union Geothermal Company of New Mexico. Do not attempt to enter these locked buildings as they are in dangerous condition. In the early 1970s several exploratory geothermal wells were drilled in this area, and from 1973 to 1982 Union Oil partnered with Public Service Company of New Mexico (PNM) to further explore the commercial potential of geothermal power. The US Department of Energy joined forces with them in 1978, hoping to build a power plant. Unfortunately, the steam pressure produced was not nearly enough for the partners' ambitions, and public outcry over environmental concerns as well as Pueblo rights led to the abandonment of the enterprise. From here the remnants of geothermal exploration are evident, with old wellheads, cut hillsides, and abandoned access roads for nearly 1 mile. The large

Contouring along Redondo Mountain.

concrete retaining wall is all that remains of what would have been the geothermal power plant. The main trail is very obvious through this section, and the abandoned side roads are easily ignored.

At about 4 miles the valley narrows and the trail passes a small burned area on the left (west). In another half mile the trail begins to climb very steeply, becoming rocky and extremely aerobically challenging for bikers. From here to the top of the climb, sulfur smells from the creek may be noticed, although any fumaroles are well hidden. At 4.7 miles the grade increases further as the trail skirts a section of threatening standing dead trees, and in another tenth of a mile the trail begins to switchback its way up the hillside, at 5 miles passing an old well platform with nice views to the right (southwest) before finally leveling out and reaching the junction with VC0302 at 5.25 miles. This is marked with a brown post, but it is easy to miss. Mountain bikers who wish to connect with Valle Jaramillo Loop (83) should continue straight (northeast) here on VC03 (see Routes for Mountain Bikers, 168).

To continue on our trail, turn right (south) at the junction onto VC0302 and follow the jeep road as it contours around the backside of Redondo Mountain. The trail is initially quite sandy and eroded, with a short stretch of deadfall, but conditions improve quickly and the trail is obvious on the ground, alternating between grass and gravel. At 5.5 miles the trail crosses another geothermal well platform, with a sulfur field to one side and nice views back down the valley to the other. After crossing the platform, the trail climbs briefly before reaching a small clearing at 5.8 miles, and then it continues to roll gently up- and downhill as it works its way toward Mirror Pond. Occasionally there is deadfall blocking the trail, but the quantity is smaller than it is on other trails in the preserve. Elk sightings along this stretch are likely.

At 6.2 miles an enormous talus field on the backside of Redondo Mountain may be seen. The trail then passes through a small aspen grove, and at 6.5 miles it crosses a shallow drainage with a pretty glade to the right (northwest). The trail becomes grassy with some encroaching locust trees, and more talus fields may be seen above you and to the left (east). After a quick downhill stretch, the trail arrives at tranquil Mirror Pond. The old timber road continues slightly further past the pond. Retrace the trail the way you came. Turn left (northwest) onto VC03 at 8.6 miles, turn right (west) onto VC02 at 12.4 miles, and return to the trailhead at 13.9 miles.

Mirror Pond.

Banco Bonito Loop

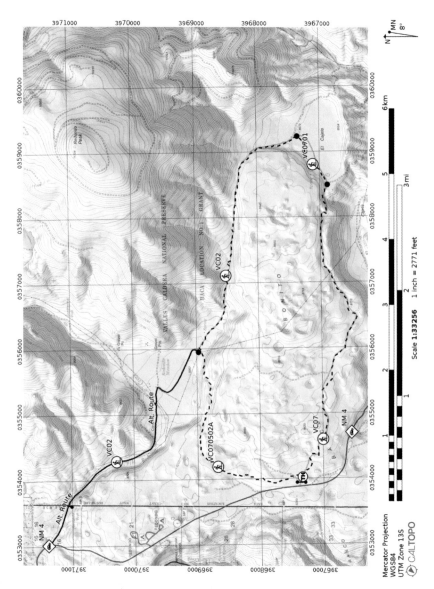

Banco Bonito Loop

A moderately challenging loop along old jeep roads passing through rolling fields of lava and stands of aspen and ponderosa and skirting the western edge of lovely El Cajete Meadow.

Distance (RT): 9.2 miles (Loop); 9.5 miles (Alt. Route with two-car shuttle); 12.1 miles (Alt. Route without two-car shuttle)

Elevation Range: 8,042–8,871 feet (Loop); 7,774–8,871 feet (Alt. Route with or without two-car shuttle)

Elevation Gain: 1,160 feet ascent (Loop); 1,150 feet ascent (Alt. Route with two-car shuttle); 1,707 feet ascent (Alt. Route without two-car shuttle)

Difficulty: Moderate to strenuous

Recommended for Mountain Bikers: Yes

Conditions: The trail is best hiked or biked counterclockwise as described below, starting from VC07 at the VCNP Banco Bonito Staging Area. The elevation gain is very gradual except for a short, sustained climb up VC070502A. This steep climb will be very aerobically challenging for bikers, who may wish to take VC02 to exit at the VCNP Redondo Meadow Staging Area (marked Alt. Route on the map). This will require either a two-car shuttle or an additional, very challenging 2.6-mile uphill return to Banco Bonito along NM 4. Some bikers may prefer to start at the VCNP Redondo Meadow Staging Area and ride clockwise, exiting at Banco Bonito and returning down NM 4. Note that this area is popular with bears, so be alert to your surroundings.

GPS is strongly recommended as the multiple, confusingly marked timber roads make navigation challenging at times, particularly on VC02; different maps of the preserve have different trails marked in different ways. Signage varies and may include named but disused side trails, yellow wooden posts, or brown posts. Note that VC070502A signage does not always include "A." Very little deadfall and a handful of eroded gullies. Hikers and bikers should not linger at El Cajete or Redondo Meadows when thunderstorms are threatening. Largely full sun in the first half, shadier in the second half. Ground conditions may be sandy, grassy, or rocky. Good opportunities for wildlife and wildflowers. Prairie dogs may be seen at El Cajete Meadow, and if you're lucky you may catch a glimpse of the feral horse that makes Redondo Meadow its pasture. Collection of plants, antler sheds, obsidian, or other items is prohibited. Disturbing any archaeological sites in the area is a federal offense.

Trailhead: At the locked cable gate marked VC07, on the southeast side of the VCNP Banco Bonito Staging Area. The Staging Area locked iron gate is near mile marker 30 on the east side of NM 4.

Coordinates: 35° 50' 20.27" N, 106° 36' 56.79" W
UTM: 13S 354072 3967292

If using a two-car shuttle, leave one car at the locked iron gate (do not block the gate) at the VCNP Redondo Meadow Staging Area. The Staging Area locked iron gate is near mile marker 28 on the east side of NM 4, at the jeep road marked VC02.

Coordinates: 35° 52' 22.36" N, 106° 37' 16.46" W
UTM: 13S 353641 3971063

Hike Details

From NM 4, turn off at the sign for the VCNP Banco Bonito Staging Area (on the east side of the highway, near mile marker 30). Park

Ponderosa pines among the lava fields.

at the locked iron gate (do not block the gate), and hop the fence, heading toward the southeast side of the Staging Area (the back right of the open area when viewed from the entrance gate). The trail starts at the locked cable gate marked VC07 and is a jeep road that begins to climb slowly through stands of ponderosa and lava fields. These are some of the youngest lava flows in the caldera, dating to about 40,000 years ago. After about half a mile there will be the first of several old, closed trails on the left (north); some of these are marked as closed and some are not, but the main trail is obvious and continues eastward.

At about 2 miles the trail passes through a recent prescribed burn area and begins a steadier climb, becoming looser and rockier and suffering from more eroded gullies. Some sections of this stretch

Aspen grove at the northwestern edge of El Cajete Meadow.

may be difficult for bikers after recent precipitation. Between dense stands of trees there are good views of the ridgeline to the right (south). Around 3 miles the lava fields are more visible, with large deposits of sparkling mica and obsidian. From here the trail is nicely treed and shadier until it reaches the southwestern edge of El Cajete Meadow.

At El Cajete Meadow, take VC0701 at the poorly marked junction with VC07 and go straight toward the meadow, then veer left (northeast). The trails are marked with brown posts, but they are not immediately visible from the junction. There is a small pond at the edge of the meadow and a few prairie dogs as well as extensive elk sign, and in wet years you may hear peeper frogs chirping away. Skirt the edge of the meadow as you head northeast, passing a natural cave formed by a lava air pocket on the left (west) at about 3.6 miles.

The trail starts to trend northward, with a view of a small saddle on the hills in front of you, and shortly after it enters an aspen grove at about 4 miles, the trail joins VC02 in a T-junction. The signpost for VC02 is slightly right (east) of the junction and a little difficult to spot. Turn left (north) onto VC02, passing through healthier stands of trees and noting talus fields on the hillsides to the right (northeast) at about 4.5 miles. The trail begins to climb gently but briefly, and after entering a burned area it begins to descend gradually. The burned trees have almost completely fallen, so very little threat of deadfall remains along this stretch. From here, the first of several unmarked and disused timber roads will join the trail from the left (south), but as before the main trail is obvious and continues westward.

The trail heads more steeply downhill at about 5 miles, becoming rockier and somewhat loose with eroded gullies, some of which are quite severe in places and may pose a hazard to bikers. The forest is denser here and there is more shade. At about 5.75 miles a stream begins to parallel the trail on the right (north), and in wet years sections of the trail may be muddy due to overflow.

Redondo Meadow.

After 6 miles the trail passes a pretty, small meadow, and in another half mile it becomes sandy and flat as it enters a healthy stand of ponderosa. At about 6.8 miles the trail reaches the confusingly marked triple junction with VC070502A, Redondo Meadow, and VC02 trails. The Redondo Meadow trail skirts the edge of the meadow and eventually doubles back up the hillside to rejoin VC070502A, although it is unmaintained and may be impassable. If returning via NM 4 or with a two-car shuttle, see the Alternative Route below. To continue the loop back to the Banco Bonito Staging Area, turn left (southwest) and take VC070502A.

Almost immediately after leaving the triple junction, VC070502A begins a very steep ascent for nearly half a mile. While the trail is clear, this stretch will be extremely challenging for all but the most fit mountain bikers. Soon after the trail levels out, at about 7.3 miles, the trail trends right (northwest) briefly, and at about 7.6 miles it begins a steep descent southwest. Signage is nonexistent and the trail is faint here, so good navigation skills and a GPS or compass are essential. After another tenth of a mile, the Redondo Meadow trail comes up from below, joining our trail from the right (north), and is marked by a brown post. Our trail continues southwestward.

At about 8 miles the trail reaches a Y-junction with VC070503. Take the left (south) fork, which is marked by a yellow wooden signpost and a brown post. Shortly after the junction is a second yellow wooden signpost, indicating you are on the correct trail. About a quarter mile later, VC0705 joins the trail from the left (northeast), marked by a brown post; continue straight (south) on the main trail. You may begin to hear traffic from NM 4 at this point.

As the trees thin out and the lava fields become more visible, at about 8.5 miles the trail heads left (south) at another Y-junction. This is not well marked, but after the junction, as the trail climbs steeply, another yellow wooden signpost is visible. In another half mile, at about 9 miles, structures at the Banco Bonito Staging Area are visible through the trees. Aim for these to reach the open area, and then turn right (south) to return to the trailhead at the locked iron gate at NM 4 at 9.2 miles.

Beginning the climb up VC070502A.

Alternative Route

If returning via NM 4 or with a two-car shuttle, at the triple trail junction of VC070502A, Redondo Meadow, and VC02, continue to the right (north) on VC02 for 2.3 miles and exit the preserve at the VCNP Redondo Meadow Staging Area locked iron gate at 9.5 miles. This is a very clear jeep road used by park rangers. If continuing back to Banco Bonito, follow the dirt road another tenth of a mile to NM 4 and turn left (south) to return to the trailhead after approximately 2.6 miles, enduring a very steep climb uphill, and reach the Banco Bonito Staging Area at about 12.1 miles.

Routes for Mountain Bikers

In addition to the routes described in the preceding chapters, there are many options for bikers who wish to take longer rides. While there is no single-track in VCNP, do not let that deter you—many fine days have been had on the old jeep roads of the caldera's backcountry. The rides are not technically demanding, apart from the occasional stretch of loose rock, although some sections can be quite steep as the roads were built for four wheels rather than two. You may encounter vehicles occasionally, as these roads are used by rangers and researchers, but it is rare. The connecting routes described below and marked on the maps following may be linked with the trails described in this book. The suggested loops are popular among local bikers and are just some of the many that may be explored. If riding into the preserve, a backcountry vehicle permit is not currently required.

Connecting Routes

VC09

The trailhead is at the eastern boundary of the preserve and may be accessed via Cañada Bonita Trail (also known as Pajarito Nordic Trail) from the parking lot of Pajarito Mountain Ski Area (3.5 miles away) or via Pipeline Trail from Los Alamos (distances vary). VC09 connects with Cerro del Medio Loop (71), Valle Toledo Loop (91), and the east–west backcountry access road. If you return via this route, note that you will face an extremely steep climb out of the caldera.

Distance: 0.75 miles (one way)
Elevation Range: 8,935–9,114 feet

VC0401

The trailhead is on the north side of NM 4, opposite the trailhead for Coyote Call & Rabbit Ridge Trails (47). It connects with Cerro del Medio Loop (71).

Distance: 2.5 miles (one way)
Elevation Range: 8,520–8,713 feet

VC02–VC03

The trailhead is the same as that for Redondo Creek–Mirror Pond Trail (155). It connects with Banco Bonito Loop (161), El Cajete Loop (59), Valle Jaramillo Loop (83), and VC06, the latter of which leads to Valle Seco on Sulfur & Alamo Canyons Loop (139).

Distance: 6.1 miles (one way)
Elevation Range: 7,844–9,559 feet

VC08

The trailhead is the same as that for Sulfur & Alamo Canyons Loop (139) and Redondo Border Trail (147). It connects with Cerro Seco Loop (127), San Antonio Mountain Trail (133), and the east–west backcountry access road. Note that Alamo Canyon Trail is currently impassable to bikers (although plans are in the works to clear this section).

Distance: 5.6 miles (one way)
Elevation Range: 8,081–8,914 feet

Enjoying a ride in Valle de los Posos (Cerro del Medio Loop, 71). Photo by Peter Dickson.

Connecting Routes for Mountain Bikers (West)

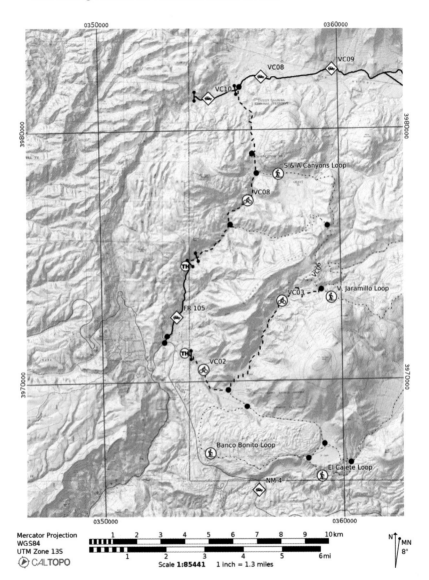

Connecting Routes for Mountain Bikers (East)

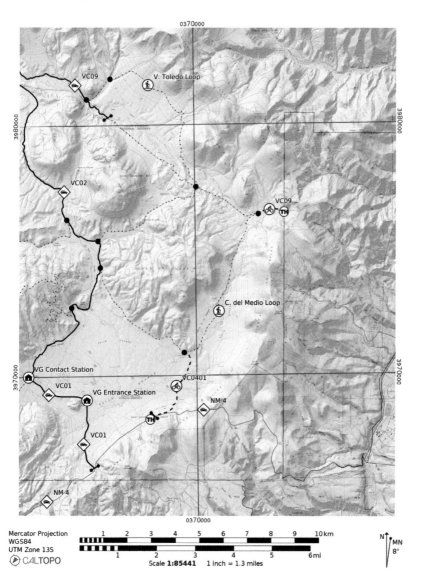

Mercator Projection
WGS84
UTM Zone 13S

Scale **1:85441**   1 inch = 1.3 miles

Suggested Loops

Cañada Bonita–VC09–VC04–VC02–VC05–VC09–Cañada Bonita

Start at the Pajarito Mountain Ski Area parking lot. Note that VC02 is open to public vehicle traffic. You will face an extremely steep climb out of the caldera at the end of the day. See Cerro del Medio Loop (71).

Distance: 22.7 miles (round trip)
Elevation Range: 8,563–9,654 feet

Cañada Bonita–VC09–VC08–VC06–VC03–VC02–VC04–VC09–Cañada Bonita

Start at the Pajarito Mountain Ski Area parking lot. Note that VC02 and parts of VC09 and VC08 are open to public vehicle traffic. You will face an extremely steep climb out of the caldera at the end of the day. See Cerro del Medio Loop (71), Valle Toledo Loop (91), Cerro Seco Loop (127), Sulfur & Alamo Canyons Loop (139), and Valle Jaramillo Loop (83).

Distance: 43.5 miles (round trip)
Elevation Range: 8,399–9,656 feet

VC02–VC09–VC08–VC06–VC03–VC02

Start at the junction of VC02 and VC03 (the trailhead for Valle Jaramillo Loop). Note that VC02, VC09, and parts of VC08 are open to public vehicle traffic. See Cerro Seco Loop (127), Sulfur & Alamo Canyons Loop (139), and Valle Jaramillo Loop (83).

Distance: 24.2 miles (round trip)
Elevation Range: 8,396–9,640 feet

VC0401–VC04–VC02–VC01–NM 4–VC0401

Start at the parking area opposite the trailhead for Coyote Call & Rabbit Ridge Trails (47) on the north side of NM 4. Note that VC02, VC01, and NM 4 are open to public vehicle traffic. See Cerro del Medio Loop (71) and Redondo & Solitario Loops (65).

Distance: 15.75 miles (round trip)
Elevation Range: 8,481–8,793 feet

ABOUT THE AUTHOR

Coco Rae has spent the last twenty years wandering the trails of northern New Mexico. She has gone trekking on five continents but still loves New Mexico's backcountry more than anywhere else. She lives in Los Alamos with her husband.